PLANT GRAPHICS

GINGKO PRESS

PLANT GRAPHICS

ISBN 978-1-58423-507-1

First Published in the United States of
America by Gingko Press by arrangement with
Sandu Publishing Co., Ltd.

Text edited by Gingko Press.

Gingko Press, Inc.
1321 Fifth Street
Berkeley, CA 94710 USA
Tel: (510) 898 1195
Fax: (510) 898 1196
Email: books@gingkopress.com
www.gingkopress.com

Copyright © 2013 by Sandu Publishing
First published in 2013 by Sandu Publishing

Sponsored by Design 360°
— Concept and Design Magazine

Edited and produced by
Sandu Publishing Co., Ltd.

Book design, concepts & art direction by
Sandu Publishing Co., Ltd.

sandu.publishing@gmail.com
www.sandupublishing.com

Cover project by Dalston
Typography in Intro and Index by Sasha Prood

Printed and bound in China

CONTENTS

PREFACE

What is the best way to communicate the "natural" today, when everyone aspires to be natural? How can a graphic designer successfully communicate eco-consciousness, natural health, and renewable energy through their design?

Plants in graphic design can be flowery and graceful, or they can hint at the health improving properties of nature. They can illustrate flavor or decorate unwanted space. Most of the time, they inform the customer that the product has natural byproducts in it.

I had my first memorable encounter with plant graphics when I bought "special teas" with my mother at Gryningen, an organic health food store in Stockholm. There were products along every wall, from the floor to the ceiling, and almost all of them had elaborate illustrations of plants on them. There were dried herbs, exotic teas, algae-extracts, kelp, vegetable stock, interesting vegetarian food, fruit drinks, essential oils and soaps with all kinds of different flavors and scents I'd never encountered before. My mother bought our Yogi Tea and we left the store.

A few years later I had my first job in a flower shop. I applied because of the intricate interior of the shop and the extraordinarily well-groomed flowers, but most of all because of the sign. The sign was illustrated with a beautiful circle of ivy leaves that wrapped themselves around the shop name. It looked so lush and alive, and I was proud to enter that door every day and carry out my important tasks of watering the plants and re-potting them. I was 12 and I decided I wanted a leaf-covered sign of my own.

When I grew up I didn't become a florist, I became a designer…with a mission.

Today, when more and more consumers are making environmentally and organically friendly choices, it is vital that fresh design reflects those values. Humanity is starting to step away from the industrial era and embrace nature instead. Brian Dougherty's book "Green Graphic Design" talks about the increasing challenge for graphic designers to create a new generation of value-based brands.

Dougherty says, "In addition to creating physical artifacts (all those booklets, brochures, and banner ads), graphic designers also help clients strategize about how to build strong brands and craft communications that resonate with their target audiences. As such, we are message makers. The messages designers make, the brands we build, and the causes we promote can have an impact far beyond the paper we print on."

Plant graphics are important because they cause us to think about nature. In a world where we consume more resources than the Earth produces on an annual basis, sustainable thinking is crucial.

Graphic designers who represent brands that embrace sustainable production should see their work as part of a mission to make the world better. If we cause consumers to change their habits and choose a sustainable product because of the design, then we might have helped change the world for the better.

Last week I went into the same health food store where, 20 years ago, my fascination with natural products began. I saw my design for Naturligtvis on the shelves - an award winning, locally and sustainably produced, organic skin and hair care brand. I realized I had come full circle! To celebrate, the next step might be creating that leaf sign… with inspiration from this book, of course.

— Saga-Mariah Sandberg, plant-obsessed graphic designer with a mission

Poster & artwork for "WOW 10" - Art book

<u>Design Agency</u> artless Inc. <u>Designer</u> Shun Kawakami <u>Illustrator</u> Tadashi Ura <u>Photographer</u> Taisuke Koyama, Shun Kawakami <u>Client</u> WOW INC.

"WOW" is a creative production that is mainly a video on advertising and promotion for the company based in Sendai and Tokyo. Five units from WOW came together to collaborate on and publish the art book "WOW10" that celebrates the company's 10 year anniversary. There are two parts of the book: the first focuses on "Reconstruction of the last 10 years" and the second is a projection for "The Next 10 years."

issue   no. b   art direction and design   design for: category   color:
                  shun kawakami   WOW Inc.   Poster   1c / Black

ISBN978-4-9903549-0-9   Published by   Art direction and Design by
Printed in Japan.   WOW Inc.   artless

Item	Artists	Date of Publication	Url
WOW 10	**WOW**	**2007**	wow10.jp
	Artless	**7/4**	
Artbook and DVD	**Graf**	**Wed**	
from Japan	**Gwenael Nicolas**		
	Masafumi Ishiwata		
	Projector		
	Yoshio Kubo		

Artwork by   Illustration by   Photography by
Shun Kawakami   **Tadashi Ura**   **Taisuke Koyama**
2007 06

ssplit   no. C   art direction and design: design by: category: color:
                   shun kawakami   WOW Inc.   Poster   1c / Black

ISBN978-4-9903549-0-9
Printed in Japan.

Published by
WOW Inc.

Art direction and Design by
artless

Item

Artists

Date of Publication

Url

WOW 10

WOW
Artless
Graf
Gwenael Nicolas
Masafumi Ishiwata
Projector
Yoshio Kubo

2007
7/4
Wed

wow10.jp

**Artbook and DVD
from Japan**

Artwork by
Shun Kawakami
2007 06

Illustration by
Tadashi Ura

Photography by
Taisuke Koyama

Guillermo Padellano
director general
gpadellano@hazel.es

López Santos 4, planta 1ª
28230 Las Rozas, Madrid.
Tel. +34 91 616 97 65
Fax +34 91 616 97 66

Soledad Calvo
directora de compras
soledad.calvo@hazel.es

López Santos 4, planta 1ª
28230 Las Rozas, Madrid.
Tel. +34 91 616 97 65
Fax +34 91 616 97 66

Teresa Polo
responsable RRHH
teresa.polo@hazel.es

López Santos 4, planta 1ª
28230 Las Rozas, Madrid.
Tel. +34 91 616 97 65
Fax +34 91 616 97 66

Tomás Romero
director de tiendas
tomas.romero@hazel.es
mobil 618756069

López Santos 4, planta 1ª
28230 Las Rozas, Madrid.
Tel. +34 91 616 97 65
Fax +34 91 616 97 66

Delphine Costenoble
merchandising visual
delphine.costenoble@hazel.es

López Santos 4, planta 1ª
28230 Las Rozas, Madrid.
Tel. +34 91 616 97 65
Fax +34 91 616 97 66

HAZEL

Design Agency Mirinda Company Art Director Marina Company Designer Marina Company, Carlos Velasco Illustrator Marta Zafra
Client HAZEL/Guillermo Padellano

HAZEL is a chain store of women's shoes and accessories. The aim was to create feminine pieces that reflected the image of a dressing room. Designers reinvented drawer liners using British style floral papers with white backgrounds. They also designed custom gift bags and gift tags for the products.

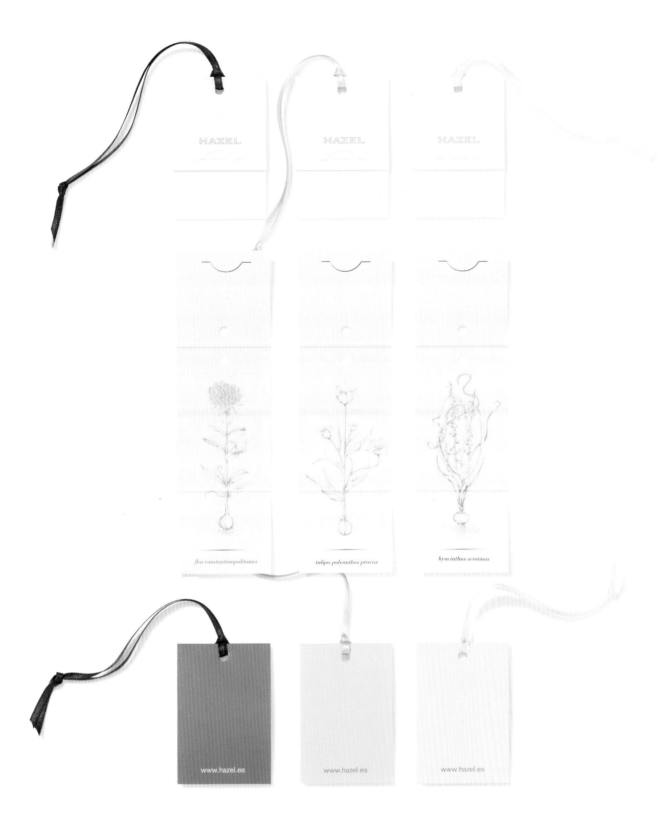

HAZEL HAZEL HAZEL

flos constantinopolitanus *tulipa polyanthos praecox* *hyacinthus serotinus*

www.hazel.es www.hazel.es www.hazel.es

中 南 香 菜
サクソフォンプレーヤー

〒640-8483　和歌山市園部1670-4
1670-4 Sonobe Wakayama 640-8483
tel: 073.454.5416　cel: 09

Kana Nakaminami Business Card

Design Agency ANONIWA Designer Naoto Kitaguchi Client Kana Nakaminami

This is a saxophone player's business card. The owner was aiming for a style that is "not just a beautiful sound, but a sound with a touch of humanity." This is the piece of work inspired by her words. To create "a sound with a touch of humanity," in place of a brush, a fine carving of plants on a plank of wood was designed to represent a life force, and it is that which was captured in the design. The business card's brief was to express the sax's shiny appearance, so the card was covered in silver-leaf.

Inside Norway

Design Agency Olssøn Barbieri Designer Henrik Olssøn, Erika Barbieri Photographer AJB Studio Client Inside Norway

Inside Norway is a branch of the Federation of Norwegian Industries that promotes Norwegian furniture design abroad. The concept of StokkeAustad was to create an abstract apple garden, as most furniture producers are located on the west coast where apple trees are plentiful and since wood still holds a central role in furniture production. The solution had to be flexible since the exhibition was to later travel to Tokyo and New York to represent different manufacturers.

During the creative process a connection became apparent between the wood material and the simple process of making the apple tree by-product of apple jam. The work consisted of silkscreened white cotton handkerchiefs tied to the branches that could easily be shaped into folded flowers that visitors could take home. Visitors were also served apple jam on freshly baked bread, sparkling wine in traditional Norwegian glass jars, and fresh apples.

We had to defeat the nature.
We had to domesticate the nature. The nature works
for us – and we are working for the nature.
First there was the tree. We wanted to create furniture.
We wanted something to sit on.
Perhaps you would like something to sit on as well?
That is why we created a chair for you.
Did you rather prefer apple jam?
Well, then you would have to make it yourself.
We made some fine chairs for you.
This is the way we collaborate so that you can sit
yourself down in a comfortable chair and enjoy your
homemade apple jam.

www.insidenorway.no

n° .... /3599

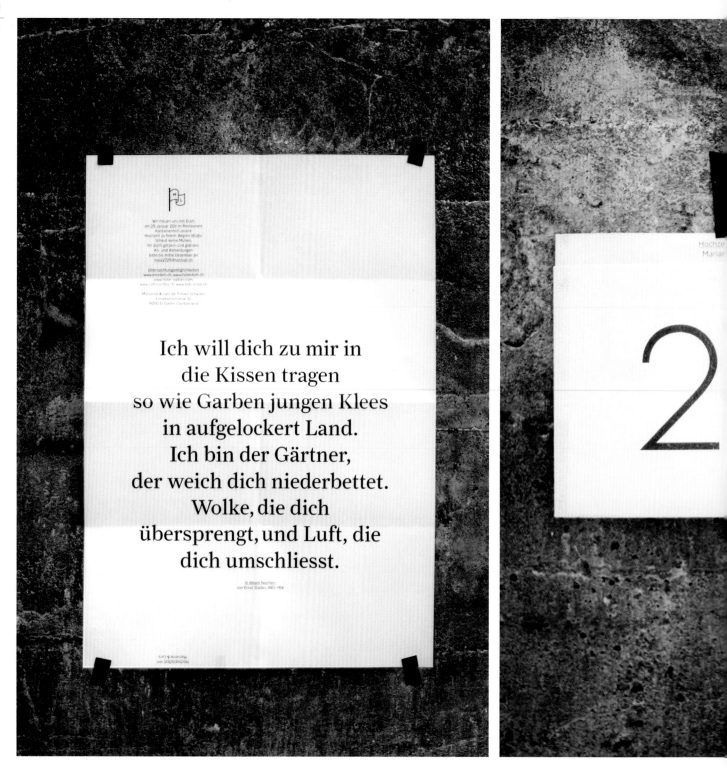

Marianne & Lars Wedding Invitation

Designer Dominic Rechsteiner Client Marianne & Lars

The project was a wedding invitation split into two parts. The first part of the design was a simple folded flier for the aperitif reception, and the second part was a folded poster with a floral engraving for the wedding. Both were sent to guests within a copper-metallic envelope. The source of inspiration for this project was the bride and groom's professions and passion for flowers.

"At This Rate" Booklet

Designer Matt Willey Photographer Giles Revell Client Rainforest Action Network

"At This Rate" booklet was produced to raise awareness of the destruction of the Amazon rainforest for the San Francisco based charity Rainforest Action Network (RAN). Each booklet is made from only one sheet of FSC certified paper, folding out from the cover into a 12-page concertina, maximizing the sheet usage and minimizing waste.

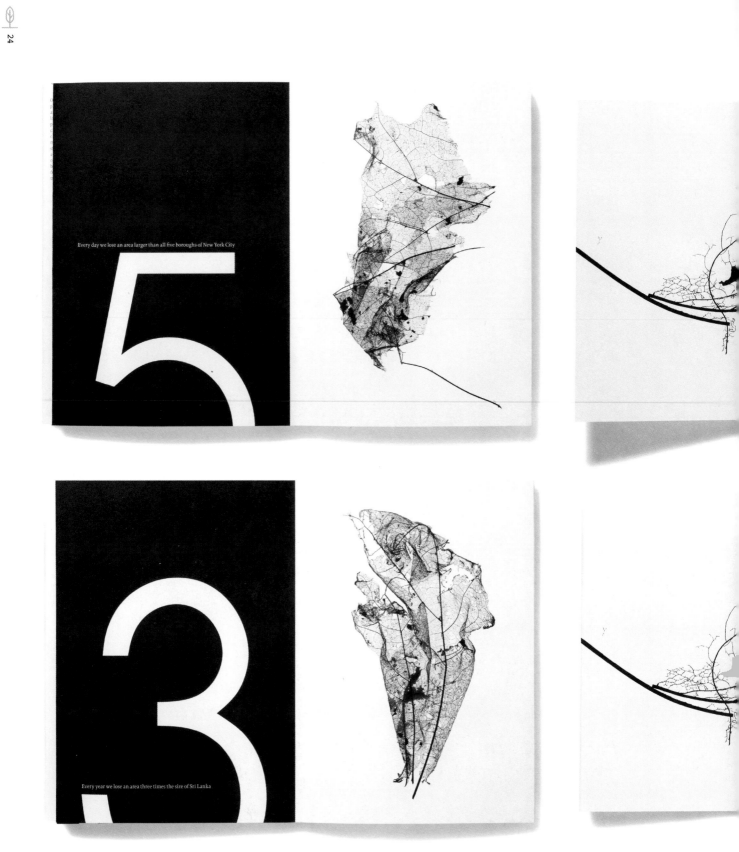

Every day we lose an area larger than all five boroughs of New York City

Every year we lose an area three times the size of Sri Lanka

Coca i Fitó negre wine

Design Agency Atipus Client Cellar Coca i Fitó

Coca i Fitó is a signature wine that is contemporary and cosmopolitan and that was introduced into the international market with a luxury value. This new concept of wine is nuanced and reflects the tastes of the wine maker.

Coca i Fitó
NEGRE

www.cocaifito.cat

★
MONTSANT
DENOMINACIÓ D'ORIGEN

JASPI blanc wine

Design Agency Atipus Client Cellar Coca i Fitó

The "blanc" is the white wine grape variety of the JASPI collection. It has a fresh character but with a touch of wood flavor, which is what the label was designed to communicate. A classic representation of the vineyard, in the same style as the rest of the collection, the label features illustrated leaves that imbue the design with freshness and color.

Ippon Matsu Beer Packaging

Art Director/Designer Kota Kobayashi Photographer Emiliano Granado Copywriter Miloš Mihajlovic Client Ippon Matsu Beer

In the city of Rikuzentakata, a single pine tree stood for a testament to survival after the tsunami of 2011. This beer's name means "One-Pine Tree" and its design is a symbol of charity and hope for a brighter future in Japan. A scroll-like handwritten label seals the top of the bottle and has a story hidden on the inside of the paper. The label is a solitary pine made of three triangles facing up, symbolizing a wish for progress in the reconstruction efforts.

Sexologist Business Card

Designer Inbal Lapidot, Tel Aviv, Isreal Photographer Karin Lapidot

The project was to design a business card for a marriage counselor and sexologist. Inbal wanted to give a sense of warmth and slight sexuality, in a gentle and subtle design. Inbal used monochromatic photos of erotic flowers with soft and suggestive shapes and tones, to convey sensitivity and passion. Photos of flowers by Ron Van Dongen.

The Initiative for Bio-Diversity in Arid Regions

<u>Design Agency</u> Paperview Design <u>Designer</u> Lorette Shebaya <u>Client</u> American University of Beirut

Paperview Design was asked by the American University of Beirut's IBSAR center (The Initiative for Bio-Diversity in Arid Regions) to design promotional items to create awareness and introduce people to a wide range of native Lebanese trees. Each tree was individually packaged as a collector's item, and stamped on the bottom with the name of the tree species. Trees were laser cut out of balsa wood and enclosed within invitation cards for the launch party. Calendars were designed that showcased orchids, Lebanese natives.

WISHING
YOU A
PEACEFUL
NEW YEAR

IBSAR has created this collection of Lebanese trees especially for
you to enjoy and reflect on the importance of nature in our lives.

IBSAR (Initiative for Biodiversity* Studies in Arid Regions) is a pioneering
center at the American University of Beirut, Lebanon.

*Biodiversity is nature in its diversity including non living elements and
diverse living forms, such as plants, animals and micro-organisms, their genes,
their habitats, and the interdependence that connects them.

ibsar
AUB

Happy Tree & Co., Ltd.

Design Agency COMMUNE Designer Ryo Ueda Copywriter Kosuke Ikehata Photographer Kei Furuse Client Happy Tree & Co., Ltd.

Commune's task was to incorporate the company's name "Happy Tree" into its identity. The company's hope is "to be a tree which stands in the middle of everybody's happiness". The answer to the identity was very simple — use "tree of happiness" as the main concept. Commune spent a lot of time figuring out how to represent the specific features of the company within this broad concept. The pop up figure of the tree was created to cast a shadow that represents the balance embodied in all things. Happy Tree mainly focuses on the cleaning industry, so a spotless, clean image was important.

Root + Branch

Design Agency KentLyons Client Root + Branch

Root + Branch is a management consultancy business that encompasses both "hard" strategic issues and "softer" process challenges. They pay particular attention to how people work together to attain focus on key issues and produce a positive influence on business performance.

Root + Branch approached KentLyons to design their identity and stationery requirements as well as their website. The identity produced is simple and clean, it evokes both the organic root and the branch at the same time. On the stationery this was represented by a deeply debossed image that appears as a root on one side of the card and as a branch on the other side of the card.

Cilsoie PRIVATE BIJOUX

<u>Design Agency</u> ANONIWA <u>Designer</u> Naoto Kitaguchi <u>Photographer</u> Yuka Yamaguchi <u>Client</u> Cilsoie

Cilsoie PRIVATE BIJOUX is a handmade accessory brand. ANONIWA represents in this logo the preciousness of the intricate, careful handiwork that is demonstrated in Cilsoie's delicate accessories. The logo visualizes the pleasure of the turning of the seasons and the memory of picking flowers blooming on the roadside - the result is a flower coronal weave. Naoto Kitaguchi paints the picture of a brand that provides a sense of spiritual happiness through the love of plants, the natural enjoyment of the slow passage of time, and the beauty of remembering a "do-nothing" day. The design of a shopping bag with a basket shape and only one handle gives the brand a certain weltanschauung.

一本一本、想い込めて編み込まれる花の冠のように、
ビンテージのビーズや色とりどりのガラス、
たくさんの工程を経て作られたアクセサリー用のパーツたちを、
一つひとつ丁寧な手仕事で紡いだアクセサリー。
日常のふとした瞬間に感じられる、
ゴージャスな意味合いの豊かさとは対照的な贅沢・ゆとり・心の豊かさを、
手触りのある、愛のあるアクセサリーを通して届けていきたい。

Cilsoie
PRIVATE BIJOUX

chamcha Asian Dining

Design Agency ANONIWA Designer Naoto Kitaguchi Client chamcha

The owner of the restaurant "chamcha" is a suntanned, organic person - a wonderful, kind, and delicate woman. "Something that has been used for many years, with a faded color, so that an elegance of values is held dear," was conceived as her logo's identity, and "While giving thanks for the blessings of nature, we send to you our bounty: 'Food,'" was developed as a concept.

The restaurant logo was designed to look like a plate with lots of food heaped on, with the ingredients "the sun," "water," and "flowers" drawn within. Like accessories that have been used for many years, ANONIWA aimed for a deep expression in tandem with an "organic" impression. Also, the silhouette of various spices used in chamcha's cooking was decoratively arranged for the graphic pattern. "While giving thanks for the blessings of nature, we send to you our bounty: 'Food'" was used throughout as the theme.

chamcha

アジアン食堂

chamcha

アジアン食堂

小畑
菜穂子

NAHOKO
OBATA

〒530-0047　大阪市北区西天満5-3-9
Tel > 06・6364・5557
Cel > 090・1485・4072
Mail > bhu-naho@sakai.zaq.ne.jp
Open > 11:30〜 / Close > 日曜・祝日

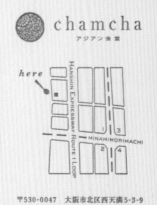

chamcha

アジアン食堂

here

HANSHIN EXPRESSWAY ROUTE 1 LOOP

MINAMIMORIMACHI

〒530-0047　大阪市北区西天満5-3-9
Tel 06・6364・5557
Open > 11:30〜 / Close > 日曜・祝日

Branding for floresta

Design Agency asatte design office Designer Satoshi Kondo Illustrator Ryoji Nakajima Client floresta inc.

This is the branding and graphic design work for the handmade doughnut shop "floresta". "Floresta" means "forest" in Portuguese. The owners of Floresta hope their doughnuts will be a favorite of customers of all ages, providing a sweet experience for families and friends. Floresta encourages these relationships and the natural world to flourish.

Satoshi Kondo designed a logo for floresta with a layer of "人" which means "human" in Chinese characters. This idea came from a character that means "forest", "森", which consists of three "木", meaning "tree".

Floresta uses natural materials to make their doughnuts, and they never use food preservatives. Satoshi Kondo expressed this process by using hand-drawn illustrations. The designer created posters to advertise a variety of themes, including posters for seasonal flavors of donuts each month and posters inviting children to enter a competition to invent new donut flavors.

floresta
nature
doughnuts
Since 2oo2 Nara

2012年夏休み特別企画

こんなドーナツ
あったら
いいな
コンテスト

「こんなドーナツあったらいいな」を
絵に描いてご応募ください。
夢のドーナツが本物になるかも。

応募期限 **8月31日**［金］まで

応募方法 応募用紙を店頭でお受け取りいただくか、ウェブサイトからダウンロードしていただき、
夢のあるドーナツや自分の食べたいドーナツなど、ご自由にお描きください。
必要事項を合わせてご記入いただき、コンテスト実施店舗へお持ちください。
ご応募いただいた方には、ネイチャードーナツ引換チケットをプレゼント！

結果発表 店頭ポスター、ウェブサイトにて［10月中旬予定］

賞 ○おいしいで賞 1名［期間限定で商品化いたします］
○いっぱいで賞 10〜20名
○永遠スタッフ賞 若干名［当店のアルバイト採用］

副賞品 ○おいしいで賞 商品化ドーナツ5個＋ドーナツ1年分
フロレスタセット［ネット、クッキー、キャンディ、ジャム］
○いっぱいで賞 ドーナツ12個＋フロレスタセット＋結果発表ポスター
［賞いっぱいで賞］ドーナツ12個＋フロレスタセット＋1年セット
○ドーナツ10個

http://www.nature-doughnuts.jp/

こんなドーナツ
あったらいいな

2010年夏休み特別企画

コンテスト

floresta
nature
doughnuts
Since 2oo2 Nara

「こんなドーナツあったらいいな」を
絵に描いてご応募ください。
夢のドーナツが本物になるかも。

応募期間 **7月1日**［木］ー **8月31日**［火］

応募方法 応募用紙を店頭で受け取りいただくか、ウェブサイトからダウンロードしていただき、
夢のあるドーナツや自分の食べたいドーナツなど、ご自由にお描きください。
必要事項を合わせてご記入いただき、フロレスタ店舗へお持ちください。
ご応募いただいた方には、その場でネイチャードーナツをプレゼント！

結果発表 店頭ポスター、ウェブサイトにて［9月実施予定］

賞 ○おいしいで賞 3名［期間限定で商品化します］○夢いっぱいで賞 5名

副賞品 ○コンテスト結果発表ポスター＋フロレスタセット［ネット、クッキー、ジャム、キャンディ、ハッサク］
○ドーナツメダル＋商品化ドーナツ5個＋ドーナツ5個［おいしいで賞受賞者のみ］
○ドーナツ10個［夢いっぱいで賞受賞者のみ］

http://www.nature-doughnuts.jp/

floresta
nature
doughnuts
Since 2oo2 Nara

くるみとフルーツ

160 yen

ラム酒に漬け込んだ4種のドライフルーツと
有機くるみをたっぷり生地に練り込みました。

期間
限定 **11・29** mon
→ **12・25** sat

floresta
nature
doughnuts
Since 2oo2 Nara

160 yen

お茶 期間
限定 **4・12** mon → **5・9** sun

希少な有機煎茶と有機抹茶を生地に練
り込んでいます。一口食べるとさわやかな
お茶の風味が広がる、素朴だけれど新鮮
なフロレスタらしいドーナツです。

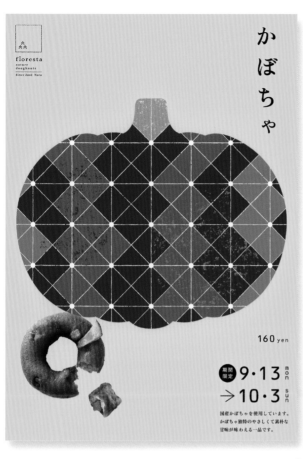

かぼちゃ

160 yen

期間限定 9・13 mon → 10・3 sun

国産かぼちゃを使用しています。かぼちゃ独特のやさしくて素朴な甘味が味わえる一品です。

160 yen

旬のフレッシュないちごがたっぷり。手作りクレームゾーンと5つぶ大の、甘酸っぱさとつぶつぶをお楽しみください。

いちごミルク 期間限定 2・15 mon → 3・14 sun

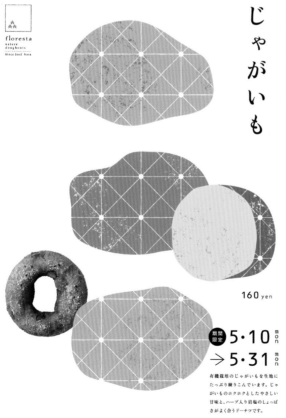

じゃがいも

160 yen

期間限定 5・10 mon → 5・31 mon

有機栽培のじゃがいもを生地にたっぷり練りこんでいます。じゃがいものホクホクとしたやさしい甘味と、ハーブ入り岩塩のしょっぱさがよく合うドーナツです。

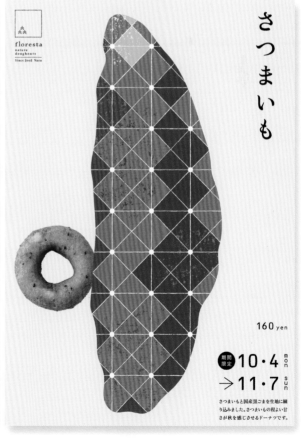

さつまいも

160 yen

期間限定 10・4 mon → 11・7 sun

さつまいもと国産黒ごまを生地に練り込みました。さつまいもの程よい甘さが秋を感じさせるドーナツです。

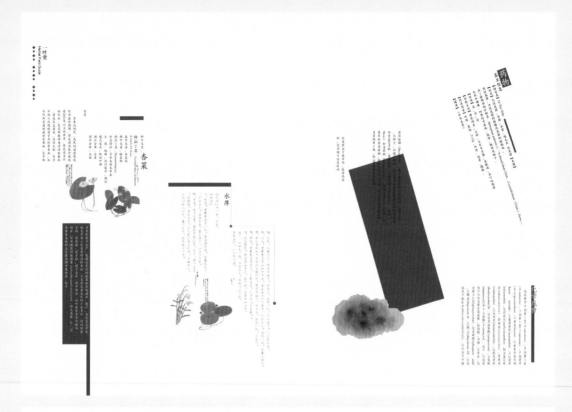

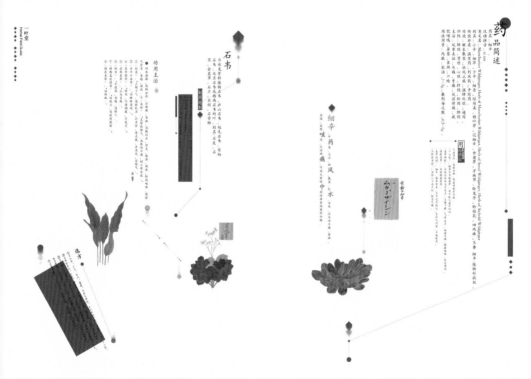

The leaf traditional Chinese medicine series design

Designer Wang Wen

This series design, including VI, packaging, and book design, embodies the taste of a variety of herbaceous plants. Designer Wang Wen tried different ways to represent the feeling of traditional herb culture, such as handwritten lettering and hand painted watercolor illustrations of each plant. She wanted to convey the Chinese style and a simple, modern and fresh taste, to attract people's attention to traditional arts and make them aware that traditional style can be imbued with new character and applied to modern issues by contemporary designers. New variations on older motifs are an important method of passing down traditional culture. Herbs and plants are the protagonists of the show, and because the theme is traditional Chinese medicine, Wang Wen added some water and acupuncture elements. The process was very interesting; Wang Wen used some old forms to shape her books. Through the process of the work, she realized that art and nature are never out of fashion.

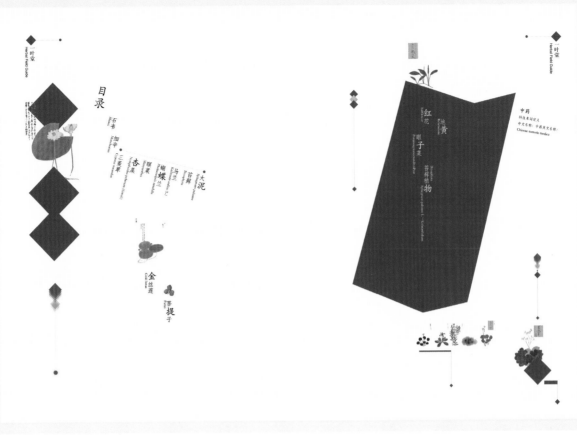

目录

中药
科技术语同定义
中文名称：中药英文名称：
Chinese materia medica

红花

地黄

嘎子菜

苔藓植物

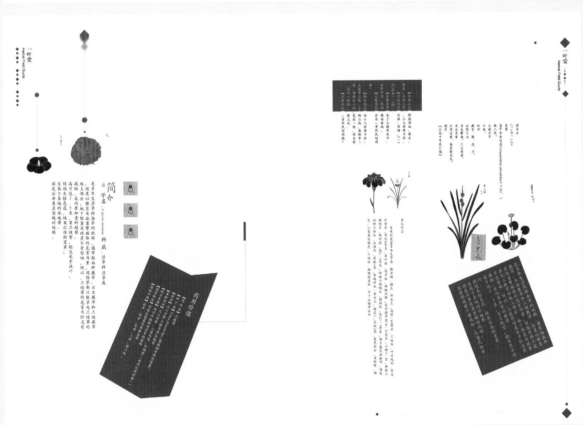

简介

学名：

科属：莎草科莎草属

是多年生莎草科统称。通常称品种属草，周围以根及根茎繁殖体的是有重。地上茎约高，中间萎基茎不易，可减弱生长。结高而萎，重三棱繁而减弱生长势。三棱繁的免害于饮没有顶端生长色花，逐渐变复，生长各地的水地带，割花后浦素复坚硬的根。

药用价值

Notes Of
The **Herb**
Medicine

Produce of: Author:
HERBFIT   Wang Hua

Herbfit

Designer Wang Hua

Herbfit is a brand of modern Chinese medicine that focuses on modernizing traditional Chinese medicine. Natural, healthy, fresh and simple brand images attract and encourage the new generation to know, use and protect traditional Chinese medicine. Herbfit brings a brand new image of modern Chinese medicine to people while retaining a strong grounding in Chinese culture. The project includes the visual identity design, package and a book introducing Chinese medicine culture through herb illustrations. Chinese medicine is introduced in an interesting way. All the products together shape a new image that keeps pace with life and introduces the younger generation to older traditional medicine.

The benefits of Cordyceps

Cordyceps may promote liver health

Cordyceps have antioxidant activities, free radical scavenging abilities and benefits in diabetes and cancers.

Anti-inflammatory, antioxidant, anti tumour, anti-metastatic, immunomodulatory, hypoglycaemic, steroidogenic and hypolipidemic effects.

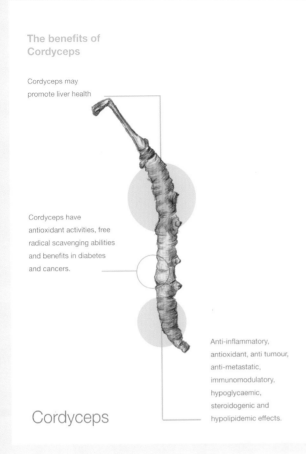

Cordyceps

High quality nutritional supplement

Tonifying lung and nourishes yin

Nourishing Stomach

Enhance metabolism, soften and smooth skin, prolong life

Bird's Nest

Promote weight loss and fight obesity

Stimulating the appetite

Stop coughing and quiet nerves

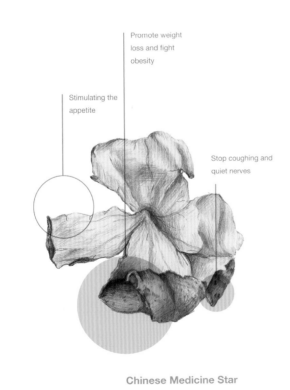

Chinese Medicine Star

Tangerine Peel

Panax ginseng C.A.Mey

Engender liquid, quench one's thirst and reinforcing Qi.

Ginseng Rhizome

Use as the emetic.
It can deliver the highest quality nutritional supplement and enhance physical strength and capacity of brainwork.

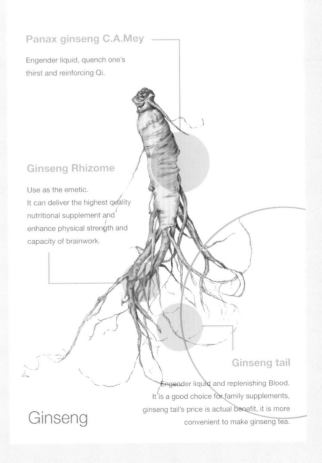

Ginseng tail

Engender liquid and replenishing Blood. It is a good choice for family supplements, ginseng tail's price is actual benefit, it is more convenient to make ginseng tea.

Ginseng

Eleven Madison Park

Design Agency e.a.d. Designer Juliette Cezzar Client Eleven Madison Park

When Chef Daniel Humm and General Manager Will Guidara came to Eleven Madison Park in 2006, they knew that they wanted it to be the best restaurant in the world. One of the first things they did was commission a new identity that would draw from the art deco elements in the dining room space and mark the restaurant's new emphasis on modern, progressive, and upscale food that was very different from the heavy French cuisine that used to be its regular fare.

The leaf forms came directly from the refurbished woodwork, and the silver foil stamp is used everywhere, keeping the look clean and light while maintaining an urban edge. One of the initial inspirations was the logo for the Four Seasons, arguably the best restaurant of the 20th century, with its four trees marking out spring, summer, fall, and winter. The identity is a single line, so it can be thin or thick depending on the size or context. The typeface was drawn by Dante Carlos and assembled into a usable typeface by e.a.d. for this project. The identity has been carried out across both print and web, and also appears on packaging and promotional products.

Hortiart

Design Agency Bunch

Bunch was responsible for creating the identity for Hortiart, a Croatian based landscaping company. The illustrations set the style for the brand and were developed for uses across a range of different applications including laser cut and foil embossed business cards and stationery.

Agromediterránea Package

Design Agency La Federal Designer Andrea Ataz Client Agromediterránea

The project was the packaging design of vegetables for an important supermarket located in Spain. Andrea Ataz designed icons for each kind of vegetables and illustrations that look like images in a kaleidoscope. The variety of vegetables is shown through bright and colorful images that transmit a feeling of nature and simplicity.

radish

oak leaf lettuce

corn

escarole

iceberg lettuce

cabbage lettuce

curly cabbage lettuce

lombard

lettuce hearts

broccoli

mint

romaine lettuce hearts

Siempreviva

Designer Clara Fernández

Siempreviva is an imaged landscape design festival in Valencia. The project included the entire graphic identity for the event. Through vectors and colors, Clara Fernández developed a broad morphology of the universe, which refers to nature in a very particular way.

IX__
ENCUEN_
TRO_DE
DISEÑO
DEL ____
PAISAJE
_

VELENCIA/
ESPAÑA

ELPAISAJE.-HOY..........---
,AQUI,-
-----UN_RECORRIDO
 POR_EL_TERRITORIO,
LANATURALEZA,
LA....
REINTERPRETACIÓN,_
LOS------RECUR_SOS,
EL.DISEÑO..__Y---
LA___REFLEXIÓN........

S I E M
P R E
V I V A

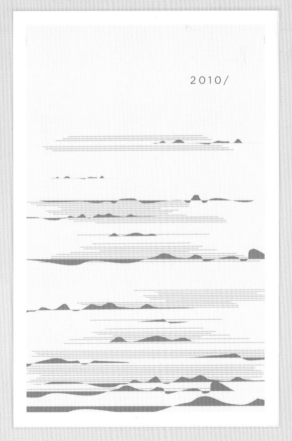

2010/

macually o'neil
pilates instructor

+31 (0)62 915 5566
macaully@breatheamsterdam.nl
overtoom 239, 1054 HV amsterdam
www.breatheamsterdam.nl

Breathe Brand Identity

Designer Crista Conaty Client Breathe

Inspired by the organic shapes of nature and the lines of Zen gardens, "Breathe" is an identity created for a yoga, Pilates and wellness studio in Amsterdam, Netherlands.

ACO HUD

<u>Design Agency</u> Dalston <u>Designer</u> Magnus Darke, Sofia Darke <u>Client</u> Patriksson PR & ACO HUD

Patriksson PR asked Dalston to design and produce an invitation for their client Aco Hud and their brand Natuvive — an eco-friendly anti aging cream.

Mitsue Tozuka Business Card

Design Agency ANONIWA Designer Naoto Kitaguchi Client Mitsue Tozuka

Business card for an interior designer. To express the client's creativity, the illustration ANONIWA drew is an antique-looking wooden chair that has been abandoned in a garden. As time passes, plants grow around it and butterflies gather, creating an earthly paradise. The sprouted plants mimic the growth, creativity, and humor of the designer. The illustration on the business card is split into four parts that can be combined to form one full picture.

戸 塚 光 恵
デザイナー

Designer / Space Interior Division

Cel: 090.9712.3937
Mail: hikarimegumu@dsk.zaq.ne.jp

mitsue tozuka

kikiki=forest

Designer Maykol Medina

Maykol Medina is obsessed with trees. He discovered that the Chinese character for "tree" (木) was an amazing icon, which visually can represent the shape of a tree. The meaning of the Japanese character ki (き) is "trees" in English, " 木 " in Chinese. If you put three trees (木) together, you will get the Chinese character " 森 ", which means "forest." When Maykol was studying Japanese he thought this linguistic discovery was so amazing that he illustrated a tree character people can understand even if they don't read Chinese. This project also shows the love and affection he has for both trees and Chinese characters, and through the project people are becoming more sensitive to the importance of trees. The meaning of "ki (き)" is "trees" in English, " 木 " in Chinese. Therefore, we can make a forest " 森 " with three "ki (き)", or " 木 ".

69

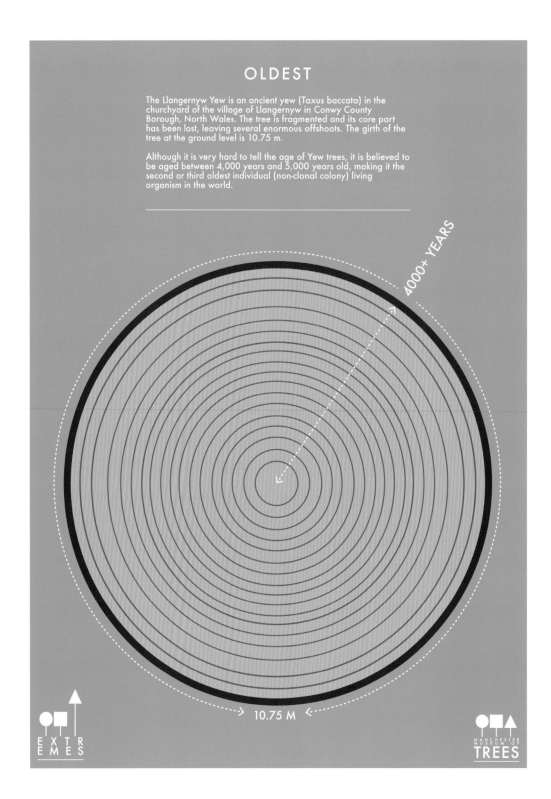

Trees

Design Agency Dan Heron Design Designer Dan Heron

"Trees" is a personal project combining Dan Heron's interest in nature and love of infographics. The initial idea revolved simply around branding a fictional museum of trees but developed into also creating an exhibition idea — the "extremes" of trees — and information graphics for this exhibition.

Having always been interested in facts and figures, Dan Heron looked into some of the record breaking trees from around the world, from the tallest coast redwood trees of North America to the oldest Llangernyw yew from Wales, and picked out the most interesting examples in order to design the infographic posters. The visual style of the project comes from a love for minimalism and simplicity within design. Dan Heron wanted the museum of trees to have a fun feel but with a modern twist.

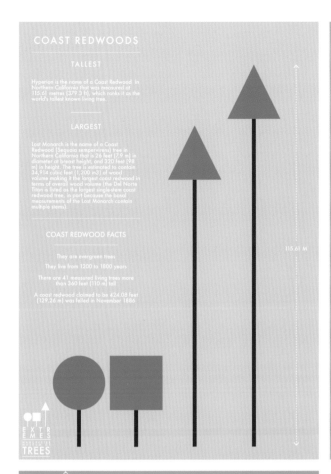

COAST REDWOODS

TALLEST

Hyperion is the name of a Coast Redwood in Northern California that was measured at 115.61 metres (379.3 ft), which ranks it as the world's tallest known living tree.

LARGEST

Lost Monarch is the name of a Coast Redwood (Sequoia sempervirens) tree in Northern California that is 26 feet (7.9 m) in diameter at breast height, and 320 feet (98 m) in height. The tree is estimated to contain 34,914 cubic feet (1,200 m3) of wood volume making it the largest coast redwood in terms of overall wood volume (the Del Norte Titan is listed as the largest single-stem coast redwood tree, in part because the basal measurements of the Lost Monarch contain multiple stems).

COAST REDWOOD FACTS

They are evergreen trees

They live from 1200 to 1800 years

There are 41 measured living trees more than 360 feet (110 m) tall

A coast redwood claimed to be 424.08 feet (129.26 m) was felled in November 1886

115.61 M

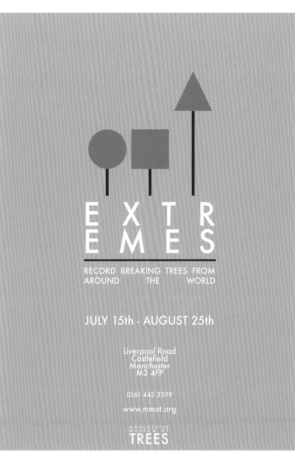

E X T R E M E S

RECORD BREAKING TREES FROM AROUND THE WORLD

JULY 15th - AUGUST 25th

Liverpool Road
Castlefield
Manchester
M3 4FP

0161 442 3399

www.mmot.org

MANCHESTER MUSEUM OF
TREES

WIDEST

The Sunland 'Big Baobab' is in Modjadjiskloof in Limpopo Province, South Africa and is famous internationally for being the widest of its species in the world. Africa is symbolised by these magnificent trees. The Sunland Big Baobab is carbon dated to be around 6000 years old.

BIG BAOBAB FACTS:

22 metres high
47 metres in circumference
Home to many bird species

The hollow inside of the tree contains a fully functioning pub and wine cellar!

There have been fires in the hollow in 1650 AD, 1750-1780, 1900, 1955 and 1990

22 M

47 M

10.64 M

Adidas originals grün

<u>Design Agency</u> Studio Intraligi <u>Designer</u> Philippe Intraligi <u>Fashion Designer</u> Camilla Veth <u>Product Designer</u> Ilka Liebmann
<u>Client</u> adidas originals

adidas originals' first green collection was launched in 2008. The collection consists of sustainable shoes and apparel made
of eco-friendly materials such as cork, recycled gum, hemp, jute, recycled EVA, wood, grass and recycled garments. Studio
Intraligi designed several patterns, icons and apparel graphics around the theme of collaged and mixed materials and made
these into sporty, fashionable clothing.

Cozy Cup

<u>Design Agency</u> Kipo Design Group <u>Designer</u> Kirill Belyaev, Polina Oshurkova <u>Client</u> Chasha Tepla

"Chasha Tepla" is a small group of people driven by the same ideas and keen on good Chinese tea. They sell and deliver elite kinds of tea in Saint-Petersburg. The name translates as a "cozy cup" or "bowl of warmth." The name reflects the warmhearted spirituality typical of this Eastern drink. The design of the product supports this feeling which is based on simple image elements: water, steam, tea leaves, cups, and fire.

The project included the creation of the name and the dynamic logo of the company, as well as the basis of corporate identity. The main elements of the design are simple images formed by thin lines, hieroglyphs, natural materials, and characteristic typography that contrast two different fonts: the grotesque font used for the name of the brand and the antique font used for the rest of the text. The business cards were silk screened on cardboard made out of 100% recycled paper.

water	steam	tea leaf	cup	fire

水　温　葉　杯　火

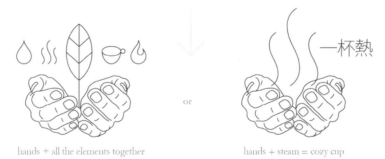

水·温·葉·杯·火

+

hands forming a cup shape

hands + all the elements together　　or　　hands + steam = cozy cup

水·温·葉·杯·火

Yiyang Black Tea

<u>Design Agency</u> Ruiyi Design Office <u>Designer</u> Hu Changfa

Visual identity for Yiyang Black Tea.

ARE
CACE
AE

TARAXA
CUM OFFICI
NALE

Plants

Design Agency Studio PATTEN Designer Aida Novoa

Editorial for a scientific magazine.

ARE

CACE

TERO   AE   TARAXA

HYTA   CUM OFF

NALE

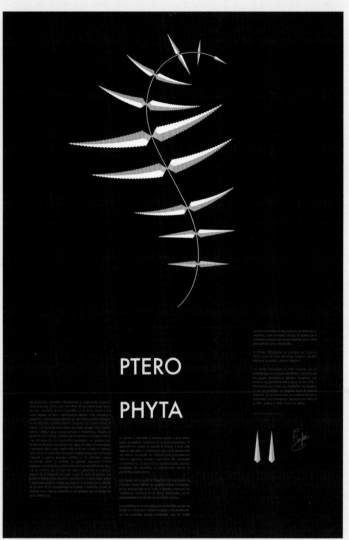

PTERO

PHYTA

KIMCHEE restaurant

Design Agency KIMCHEE Design team Creative Director Dong Hyun Kim Graphic Designer Erika Ko Interior Designer Jiweon Ahn
Photographer Yu-kuang Chou

The unique, stylized interior of this Korean restaurant in Holborn, Central London, at first glance appears very contemporary, but elements of traditional Korean culture are present throughout the interior, from the design and colour of the seasoned wooden furniture and lattice work to the stone garden and water features, which create the feeling of entering a home when customers step through the doors of the restaurant.

The brand identity therefore had to mirror this low-key design concept, and subtly draw in elements of Korean culture while still being functional and recognizable when used on a variety of materials. The concept of a traditional ink stamp using Korean characters was used for the logo, and this was versatile enough to be used across the restaurant stationery, tablemats, uniforms, and menu and web design. The green color used in the design of the logo was chosen to both match and stand out from the dark wood and stone hues and textures present throughout the interior. By using the logo consistently on a number of different materials that customers will encounter on their visits to the restaurant, customers were encouraged to remember a number of different parts of their experience. In addition to the taste of the food and the presentation of the dishes, the consistent design encourages curiosity about Korean culture and gives the restaurant a core Korean identity in the eyes of customers.

Plant a Tree

Designer Malin Holmstrom

Plant a Tree is a bag that is also a planter that holds a simple item with the capacity to make a difference - a tree. The bag will contain tree seeds, soil, and a calendar called the Earth Year Calendar. The Earth Year Calendar is a poster that encourages people to get into the routine of environmental awareness. Information about how to plant a tree is placed on the inside of the container, so as not to waste any paper.

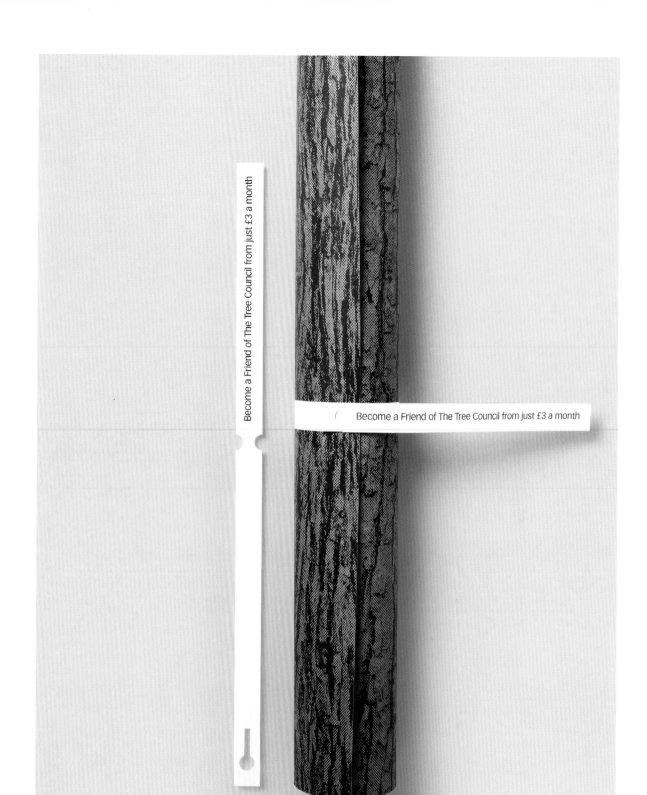

The Tree Council - Friends of The Tree Council campaign

Design Agency MARC&ANNA Designer Marc Atkinson, Anna Ekelund, Connie Wright, Dario Utichi Client The Tree Council

Tree Council is a small organization that facilitates the planting of trees through grants, campaigns and their Tree Wardens. Amongst its many member organizations are the National Trust, English Heritage and Woodland Trust. The organization is a charity, and as such struggles for money. MARC&ANNA were asked to create a campaign to promote their new Friends of The Tree Council scheme, set up in order to increase donations.

Strong and cheeky copy draws attention to the importance of trees, and the ongoing difficulties of The Tree Council. Awareness of the organization and what it does is low, so MARC&ANNA focused the copy on trees, aiming to initially attract those who were already passionate. With a printed bark texture on the reverse to resemble a tree when rolled up, posters are secured with a tree name tag to hold them closed.

Become a Friend of The Tree Council from just £3 a month

Become a Friend of The Tree Council from just £3 a month

Become a Friend of The Tree Council from just £3 a month

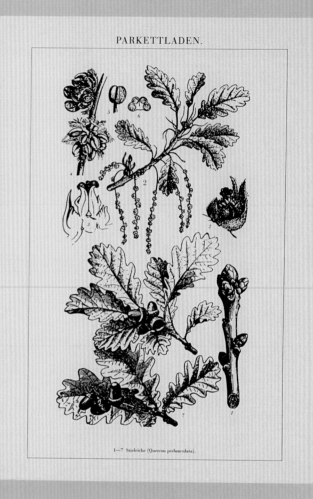

Parkettladen

Designer Esther Rieser Client Parkettladen

Corporate Identity for a parquet company, with focus on high quality parquet.

PARKETTLADEN.

1. Stieleiche (Quercus pedunculata).

Japan
for
Ecology

Japan for Ecology

Design Agency Shinmura Design Office Designer Norito Shinmura Copywriter Hiroshi Uehara Photographer Kogo Inoue
Client Japan Graphic Designers Association

Around the time Norito Shinmura was thinking of ideas with the environment as the theme, he caught sight of the Japanese national flag, and thought it looked like the "burning red of hot iron". Norito Shinmura felt it represented the continuing growth and development of Japanese industry. The red circle is covered with green leaves in his design that encourages putting as much effort into the environment as has been put into Japan's industry. He looks forward to the day when Japan fully values nature.

The forest is
a hospital of the earth.

森は、地球の病院です。

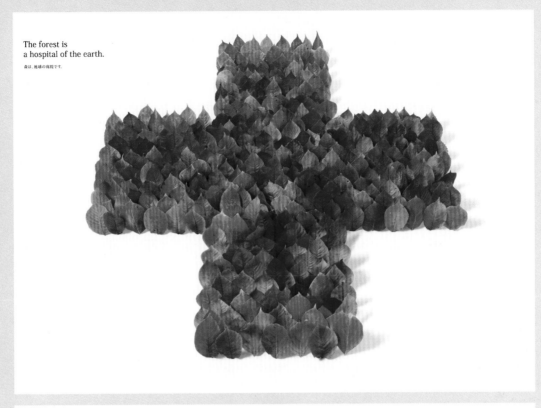

The forest is
lungs of the earth.

森は、地球の呼吸器です

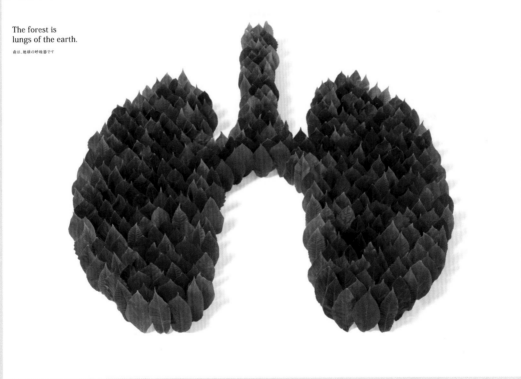

Forest Protection

Design Agency Shinmura Design Office Designer Norito Shinmura Copywriter Hiroyuki Koyama Photographer Takashi Sekiguchi Client
Forest Culture Association

"Forests are the lungs of the earth."
Forests protect the earth by changing carbon dioxide into oxygen.
The earth can only live because forests exist. Norito Shinmura created an image of lungs by arranging 400 leaves from trees.
"Forests are the pharmacies of the earth."
The earth will no longer function if carbon dioxide increases too greatly. Forests heal the earth, so they are like its
pharmacies. Norito Shinmura also designed a Red Cross symbol to express this idea, through the arrangement of 400 leaves.

P.I.Y "Plant It Yourself"

Designer P.NITTA Nutsatit

P.I.Y (Plant it Yourself) encourages cooking, creativity, eco-friendly materials, and new and positive ways of looking at things. The design of these seed containers reflects the idea that fruit and vegetables can form the base of an artistic meal. The garden itself is a colorful design and creation that each person can tailor to their own environmental and artistic beliefs.

RED ONION

BROCCOLI

RED CABBAGE

MINT

MINI TOMATO

EGGPLANT

Postage-paid padded envelopes

Design Agency Bold Stockholm Designer Oskar Lübeck Final Art Torbjörn Krantz, Oscar Söderberg Illustrator C.A.M Lindman
Client Posten AB

Swedish design agency Bold was asked to create a new packaging concept for postage-paid padded envelopes to be sold all over Sweden by the Swedish Postal Service. The brief included one concept for autumn/winter and an additional concept in the same series for spring/summer.

Bold developed a concept inspired by the look of old Swedish school posters. These first two envelopes focus on Swedish flora and use beautiful hand painted illustrations to create a pattern. The spring/summer edition shows all of the Swedish landscape flowers and specifies the names in Swedish and Latin. The envelopes have exceeded the sales targets three times over.

Möoi

Design Agency SeventhDesign Designer Bruno Siriani Client Grupo Multifood

Möoi is part of a brand new concept in Buenos Aires: contemporary food. The project uses modern art and design to build a nice, comfortable space that utilizes many different textures.

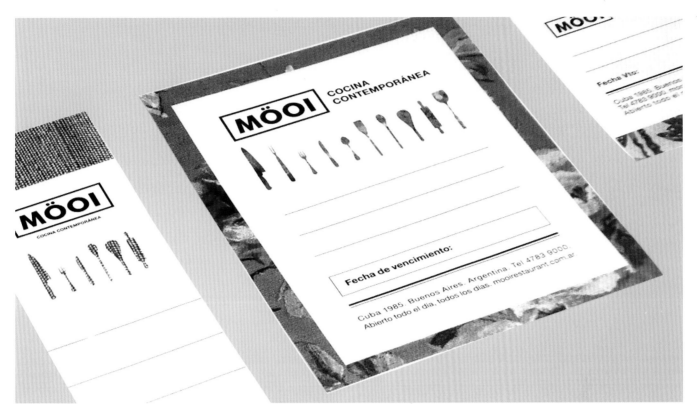

Hayford & Rhodes Identity

Design Agency Company Designer Alex Swain, Chrysostomos Naselos Illustrator Farida El Giza Client Hayford & Rhodes

London's oldest florist Hayford & Rhodes asked Company Design Agency to design their new identity when three sisters took over the business in 2008. The brief was to design a contemporary and classic look that would express strong English values. They commissioned illustrator Farida El Giza to paint four classic English flowers which were used across the identity.

Bangalô Boutique de Flores

Design Agency Estúdio Alice Client Bangalô Boutique de Flores

Bangalô — Boutique de Flores is a flower shop based in Chapecó, Brazil, which specializes in high end products and services. It's a new enterprise which aims to clearly differentiate itself from all the flower shops in the area. With this in mind, Estúdio Alice strove to represent it graphically.

The agency opted for a drawing of an exotic flower with gentle, delicate, and feminine attributes. An organic and handcrafted method was used to create the finished applications and textures. To finish the job, Estúdio Alice created a branding system which Bangalô can use on its packaging and shopping bags for a final customized touch.

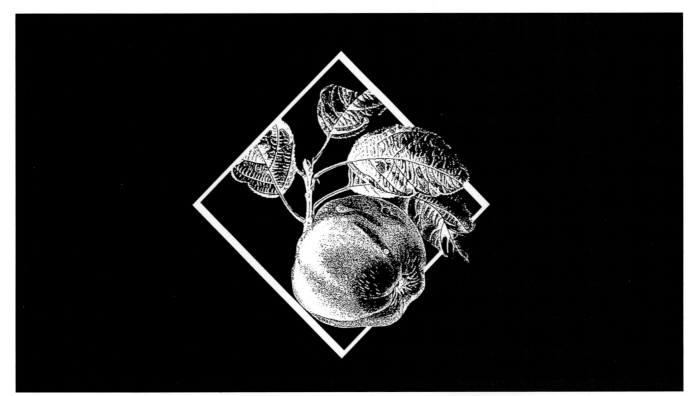

Alternateve - Vintage clothing - Branding

Designer Vanessa Pepin

Branding proposition for Alternateve, an online vintage clothing shop.

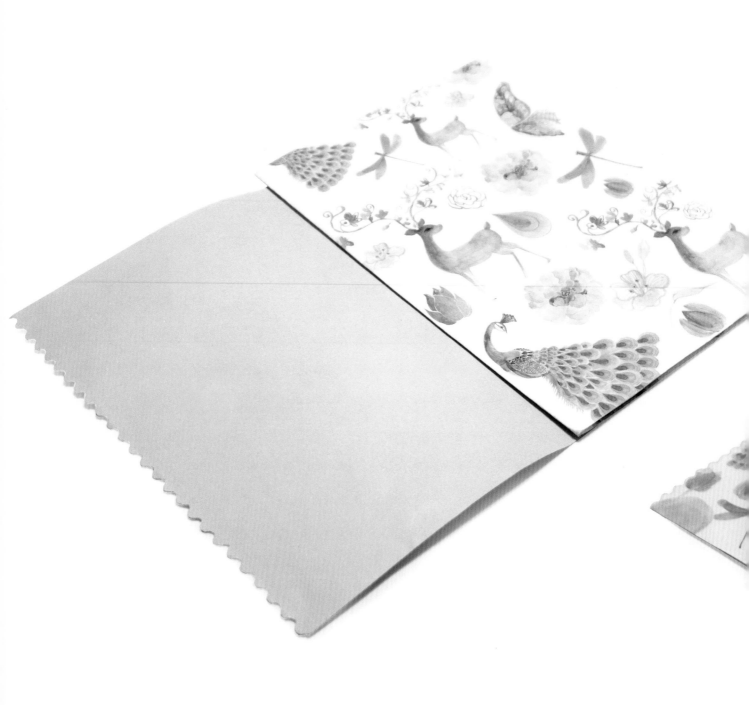

Beautiful Times SPA

Design Agency RONCHAM DESIGN OFFICE Designer Kelvin Qu Illustrator Coco Ma Client Beautiful Times SPA

Women are more beautiful than the most exotic flower. Beautiful Times is a high-end SPA club aimed exclusively at women. The SPA utilizes images of flowers, butterflies and deer to create an ambiance of beauty and tenderness, in line with its brand identity. The color of the brand is "beautiful green" which is used to create a memorable and distinctive brand experience.

The Bowerbird Group

Design Agency Longton Designer Michael Longton Client The Bowerbird Group

The Bowerbird Group is a fashion distributor located in Melbourne, Australia. The aim of the identity was to position the company as fresh and inspiring while still reaching a broad audience.

MAHO

Design Agency Zdunkiewicz Studio Designer Krzysztof Zdunkiewicz Client MAHO

Branding for the new fashion accessory brand MAHO, based in Poland. MAHO in Japanese means magic. The design is minimal, with modern typography and flower patterns as the background. All of the backgrounds are muted so that the brand name is prominent. The project targets young women who are interested in fashion and live in big cities.

IN THE CUP

ALL YOU NEED TO KNOW

25 march_
15 june

IN THE CUP

ALL YOU NEED TO KNOW

25 march_
15 june

In the Cup

Design Agency Studio PATTEN Designer Aida Novoa

Invitation for an annual reunion.

This
is
Fiction

by
Megan
Hart
directed
by
Shelley
Butler

This is Fiction, 2012

Designer Lisa Hedge Client inViolet Rep

Artwork for a theater production.

While creating the artwork to announce and advertise the theatrical performance "This is Fiction," Lisa Hedge devised a number of illustrations that were inspired by visual symbols that appear throughout the narrative of the play.

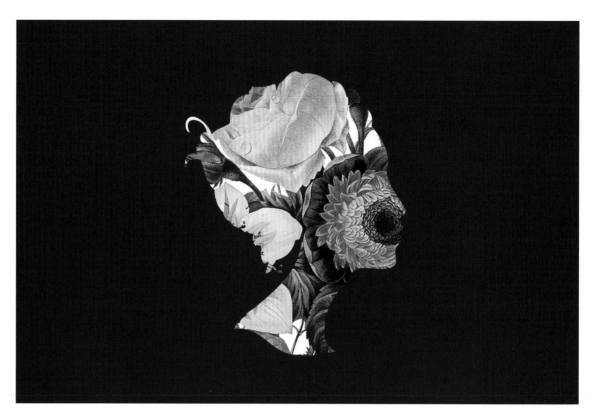

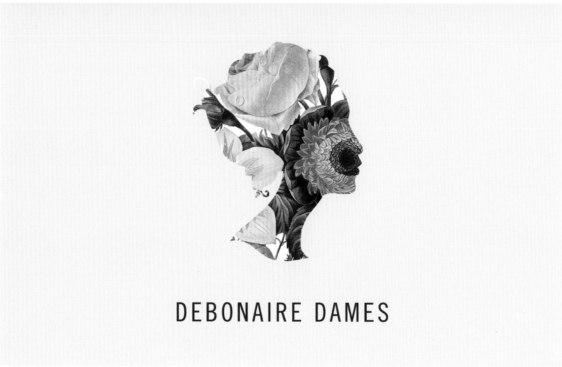

DEBONAIRE DAMES

Debonaire Dames

Design Agency Andrews&Co. Designer Sarah Andrews Client Debonaire Dames

Andrews&Co. was invited by client Debonaire Dames — a beautician based in Bunbury, Western Australia — to visualize a unique and simple brand for its new venture. Andrews&Co. worked in collaboration with the owner to source inspiration for the creative aspect of the brief from the salon, its clients and the owner's history and philosophies. Embracing the nature of the organic and natural services provided to women in a home environment, Andrews&Co.'s unique solution delivers a beautiful and fitting brand for this successful organization.

Botanica Identity

Designer Jessica Pitcher Client Botanica

Botanica is a small florist based in inner city Melbourne. The identity created references, and is a celebration of the vibrant colors that are found in the botanical world. The result is a bold identity using pattern, exaggerated color and a clean typographic approach.

BOTANICA

CHERRIE MIRIKLIS
Florist

241 Smith Street
Fitzroy Victoria 3065
T +03 9653 9471
F +03 9653 9476
c.miriklis@botanica.com.au
www.botanica.com.au

HAPPY VALEN- TINES DAY

241 Smith Street
Fitzroy Victoria 3065
T +03 9653 9471
F +03 9653 9476
info@botanica.com.au
www.botanica.com.au

BOTANICA

Botanical Save the Date

Designer Lisa Hedge

Lisa Hedge created this card to announce the wedding of two dear friends. In it, natural botanical forms are arranged within an artful scheme of constructed symmetry inspired by the wedding's floral motifs and are balanced with minimal typography.

SAVE THE DATE
FOR THE WEDDING OF

SCOTT FERGUSON
&
SARAH LANE

SATURDAY, NOVEMBER 17TH, 2012

LOS ANGELES,

FORMAL

Taylor Black branding

Design Agency interabang Designer Adam Giles, Ian McLean Client Taylor Black

Handmade in London by designer Philippa Black, Taylor Black's jewellery is characterized by its contemporary take on classic jewellery such as solid perfume lockets and charms, all with a signature rose clasp. The signature rose became the key to the identity and is reflected in the crown emblem and imagery. The vintage feel was highlighted through the use of original Victorian botanical illustrations, which were intensely cropped to give them visual tension.

EPB New Identity

<u>Design Agency</u> EPB - Espacio Paco Bascuñán <u>Designer</u> Bea Bascuñán, Albert Jornet

EPB - Espacio Paco Bascuñán studio has gone through many different stages and this project corresponds to the necessity of giving a new and fresh look to their space and identity. EPB has always been keen on flowers and nature; in fact its past identity talked about different types of orchids and their incredible characteristics. Besides, EPB has a beautiful and green garden in the studio, which is a constant inspiration for projects and for this one in particular.

This time EPB decided to get inspired from nature but in a more "artificial" way, so as to make the identity fresher and more optimistic (which was one of their aims). This kitsch side of the identity was achieved using cutout picture cards and stickers inspired by floral stickers to create new compositions, one for each season. These compositions were used as a pattern on the brand, stationery and wrapping paper. Different parts of the composition can be altered and played with so they can be adapted to different needs. The end result is a very optimistic, playful and easy going identity — characteristics that EPB as a team and as a graphic design studio also possess.

EPB / Espacio Paco Bascuñán / Diseño & más

EPB / Espacio Paco Bascuñán / Diseño & más

EPB / Espacio Paco Bascuñán / Diseño & más

EPB / Espacio Paco Bascuñán / Diseño & más

Garderobbery

Design Agency Ampersand Creative Agency, LLC Designer Natalia Churina, Pavel Iluk Client fashion start-up

Brand identity for the online shop, which offers its customers a new concept of fashion test driving.

The logo was found in the closets, wardrobes, and drawers and inspired by buckles and keylocks. When the forms were generalized through calligraphic strokes, a "G" symbol was created and was used to stand for the brand name "Garderobbery."

The solution created by using vivid textures against a black background was directed to enhance the effect of emotional elevation. The textures may change from season to season and from collection to collection. It was decided that the start of the project would be accompanied by vivid floral textures, which may be replaced by conservative geometrical forms at a later date to give the brand new life. The most important thing is that the brand can be easily managed; it is practical and designed to keep up with world trends for a long time.

Jessica Comingore Studio Rebrand

Designer Jessica Comingore

Approaching the rebrand for the studio, Jessica took the opportunity of not working with a client to push the envelope and design something unique that would be a strong visual representation of her aesthetic. Consistently inspired by the colors and textures found in nature in all facets of her work, she stumbled upon this vintage floral print and challenged herself to use it in a timeless way. Since the floral print is traditional by nature, she contrasted the pattern by duplexing a clean white front with a letterpressed sans serif to take it in a more modern direction. The JCS logo is also letterpressed atop the pattern in the same metallic gold ink used on the front of the card. The result is an eye-catching leave-behind that speaks to her love of refinement with a hint of femininity.

601 Artbook Project 2008

Design Agency 601bisang Designer Park, Kum-jun

The "601 Artbook Project 2008" competition posters revolve around the theme "Nature and Humanity". The 3-part series consisting of "Imagine?", "Breathe...", and "Fly!" embodies the interaction between and the harmony of nature and humanity. In addition, each poster in the series corresponds to the others as though to represent the circle of life. The "601 Artbook Project 2008" exhibition posters were created by overlaying the new design on top of the first competition posters. The posters deliver the theme of the event — "Artbook is conversation." — by presenting two animals from a popular Korean folktale engaged in dialogue. The human figure is in harmony with its natural surroundings.

K & K Designbuero Branding Identity

<u>Design Agency</u> K & K Designbuero <u>Designer</u> Manuela Weiß, Nadine Wittmann

The visual identity of "K & K Designbuero" changes four times a year, depending on the seasons. Basic elements are photographs of plants and trees. For every season, they create a symmetrical pattern. The concept: Looking into the exciting world of a kaleidoscope and surprising clients in regular intervals. The striking season motifs are rounded off by the simple word mark "KLECKERN & KLOTZEN". Manuela Weiß and Nadine Wittmann produced their own letterhead stationery including business cards, stamp and presentation templates.

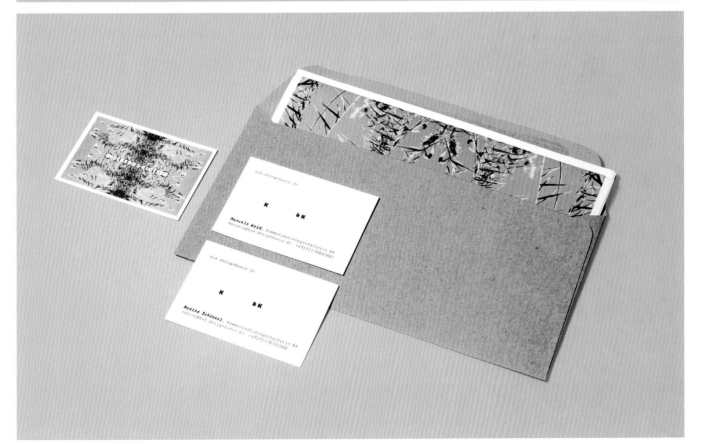

Almo Office

Design Agency Company

Company worked on the redesign of the Almo brand identity in 2007 and the relationship continued until 2012. Almo has had a sustainable approach to their business since the 1980s which was part of their brief when designing the new delivery packaging.

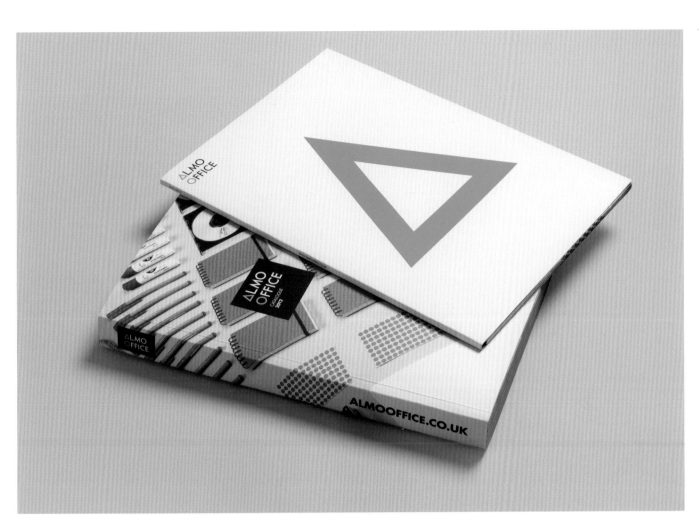

Tomer Zafrani Naturopath ND Identity

Designer Amit Sakal Client Tomer Zafrani

Tomer Zafrani is a naturopath ND, who provides treatments like: naturopathy, nutritional counseling, treatment and diet by blood type, reflexology, and more.

The founding values of the identity are reliability, health, accessibility and connection to nature. In the identity design, Amit Sakal decided to link the work of Tomer with the plant world because of the common elements and connections. The choice to design a variety of different and changing icons is based on the simple fact that Tomer's work contains many sub-areas. The color scale selected is also associated with the plant world and green atmosphere while appealing to the young audience, one of the most important targets, because handling problems early can prevent more serious problems in old age.

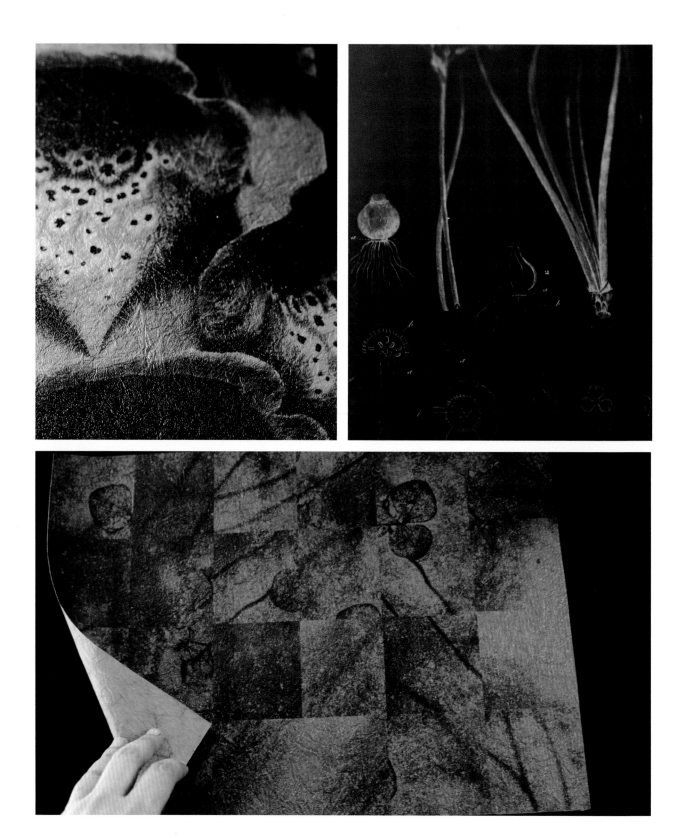

Euphoria

Designer Danielle Shami Client Shenkar Department of Visual Communication, Israel.

"Life is wasted on the living" - Identity for a flower shop specializing in poisonous plants. The idea is to take the essence of the plant or flower and create a small easy-to-carry package, so anyone can carry their poison with them. To keep death so close and yet untouchable, you carry your own death, and are reminded of life. The feeling of Euphoria works like a drug and lets the individual do anything he or she ever dreamed of doing, every little sin, every desire. The only information on the package is the chemical compound of different extracted poisons, the product's name, the logo, and the number.

Different techniques were used for this project, and every image was made on a different and unique paper with a different treatment. This project was created during an "Identity" course under the guidance of Nurit Koniak.

NARCISSE jonquille.
NARCISSUS jonquilla,

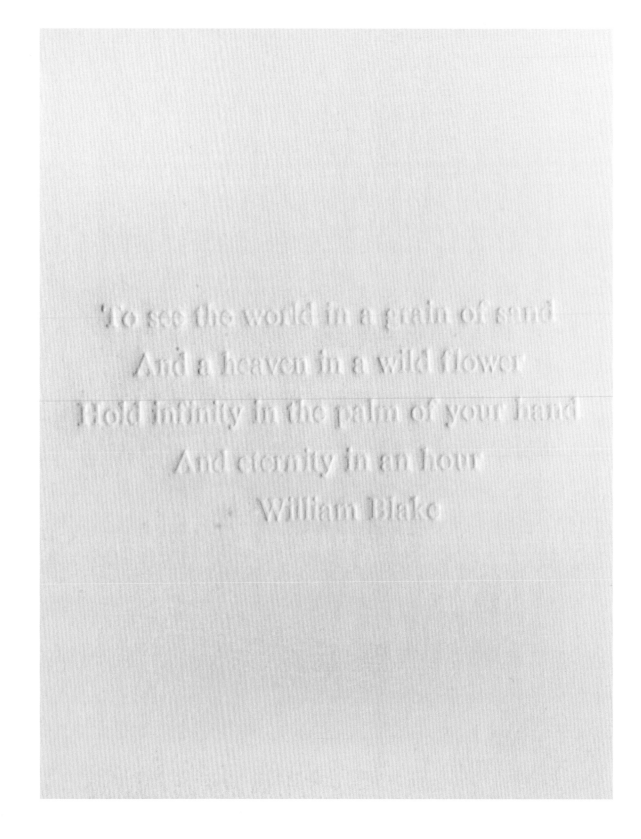

To see the world in a grain of sand
And a heaven in a wild flower
Hold infinity in the palm of your hand
And eternity in an hour
— William Blake

Flowers are Blooming under Your Skin

Designer Di Suo Photographer Yan Wang

"Flowers are blooming under your skin" represents a female with organs composed of plants. As one of nature's creations, the human body is elegant as well as fragile. Being aware of the similarities between human beings and botanical species is an excellent way to encourage self-respect and respect for our natural environment.

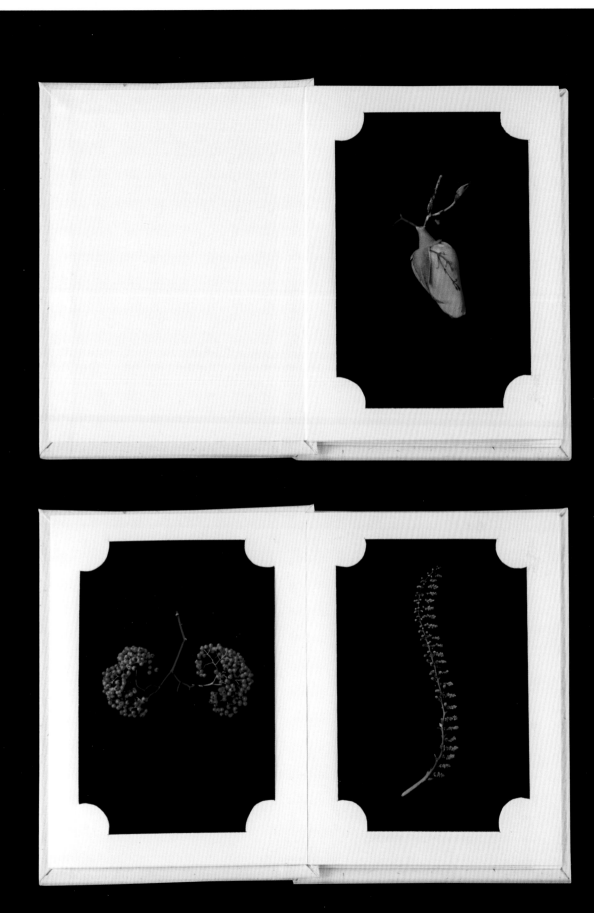

 local
wine

 female
winemaker

 critics'
choice

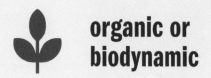 cult
wine

organic or
biodynamic

things to eat

THE LOCAL VINE™

The Local Vine Menu System

Design Agency Turnstyle Designer Ben Graham, Jason Gómez, Lesley Feldman Client The Local Vine

The Local Vine seeks to capture the essence of wine, while at the same time dissolving the pretension associated with the wine business. In Turnstyle's first meeting with the founders, the client had only one stipulation with regard to the identity: "No grapevines, wine glasses, or wine bottles." They wanted something fresh and clean without the trappings of traditional wine-based identities. Ironically, Turnstyle's solution involved cropping grapevines into silhouettes of wine glasses and wine bottles. Turnstyle reinvented these clichés to create a design that balances modern simplicity with freshness and character.

by the glass

THE LOCALVINE

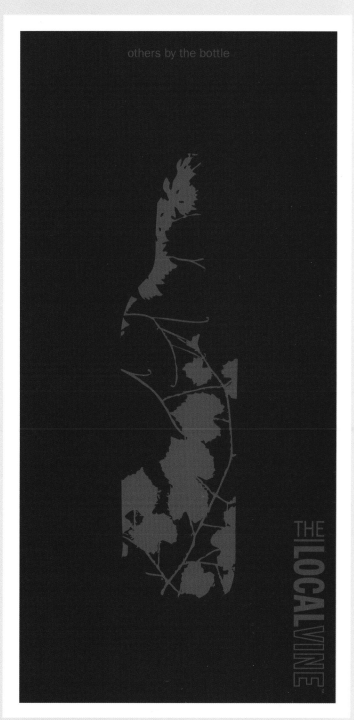

others by the bottle

THE LOCALVINE

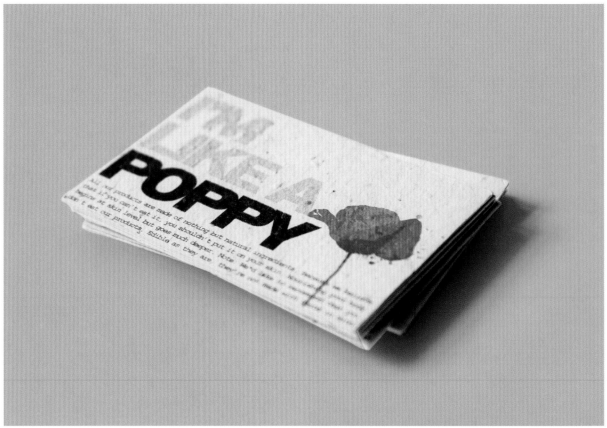

C. Cosmetics and Care

Design Agency byRosa Designer Rosa de Jong Client C.Cosmetics and Care - Caroline van Eeuwijk

C. Cosmetics and Care is a beauty shop located in Amsterdam that carries only products made of natural ingredients. For this project, Rosa tried to stay as close to the product as possible. Normally women don't think about the fact that everything you put on your skin ends up entering your body. This is why the identity contains different kinds of paper that can all be put back into nature or be eaten and bring nothing but good things. To bring this to life, business cards were made of both edible paper and "seed paper", which sprouts wildflowers if you plant it into the ground.

Along with this idea and design, Rosa wrote a brand story to be featured on the bottom of C's business cards to explain where the idea came from. The right paper and textures for the entire identity were very important and go along with the very beautiful interior design of the store by Anne Brouwer. Together the store design and identity design create a very classy and luxurious look for the brand.

Milton Deforge Impression Corporate ID

Design Agency Ultra:studio Designer Ludovic Gerber Client Milton Deforge Impression

Milton is a great printer whose fine print work is sensitive and accurate. The flowers are ideally suited to the colorful print world.

CHOW TAN TAN

Design Agency Designdo Brand Design Consulting Organization Designer Guanlin Li, Gang Long Client Chow Tan Tan Apparel

CHOW TAN TAN is a contemporary garment brand established in 2006, which emphasizes crafts and quality. The fashion industry's constant rapid creative process has resulted in many independent fashion brands. Within this competitive market, CHOW TAN TAN has taken steps to differentiate itself from competitors while meeting needs of consumers and having a clear vision. Designdo Brand Design Consulting Organization positioned CHOW TAN TAN as a brand that creates harmony and pursues nature and purity. The designers channeled an artistic concept of nature into the visual identity to create a peaceful and comfortable atmosphere. The package has an air of simplicity and the paper treatment appears luxurious.

Xmas Cards 09: Leaves

Designer Nicholas Jeeves

In 2007, in response to the amount of waste paper generated every Christmas, Nicholas Jeeves decided to only use found or re-used materials for his Christmas cards from then on.

First using waste printers' board (2007) and then pages from an antique Dickens book (2008) for his cards, in 2009 Nicholas carefully collected fallen leaves during his travels, and then stamped and numbered each of them. It took the whole autumn to collect all 100 leaves — the designer wished for each of them to be perfect specimens. The leaves were then sealed in polybags that were otherwise headed for destruction.

Each leaf bears a black circle with the text:

CENTRE
D'OSTEOPATIA
I TERÀPIES
GLOBALS

COTG. Corporate Identity

Design Agency Estudi Conrad Torras Designer Conrad Torras Boldú Client COTG

Corporate identity for the Center for Osteopathy and Global Therapy (COTG). The underlying concepts of this project were the search for a natural equilibrium and the parallels between trees and the branching systems of the human body (e.g., the circulatory, lymphatic and nervous systems).

Osteopathy emphasizes the interrelationship between all the different circuits of the human body and believes that they are all connected. The human body is formed and works like a tree. The leaves graphically represent different types of trees and a connecting network, and every different type of leaf also represents a human body. The final outcome is a very personal, fresh, organic, and calm identity with many applications.

CENTRE D'OSTEOPATIA I TERÀPIES GLOBALS

PTGE. FERRAN LLÀCER 22, 3ᴿ 2ª
08208 SABADELL (BARCELONA)
TELÈFON / FAX. 93 725 31 48
INFO@COTG-OSTEOPATIA.COM
WWW.COTG-OSTEOPATIA.COM

FERRAN TRINIDAD
OSTEOPATIA, FISIOTERÀPIA-RPG,
LLICENCIAT EDUCACIÓ FÍSICA
FERRAN@COTG-OSTEOPATIA.COM

DRA. PILAR PAU
MEDICINA-HOMEOPATIA
COL. 32.883
URGÈNCIES: 656 394 879

ANGELS TORRAS
OSTEOPATIA
ANGELS@COTG-OSTEOPATIA.COM

FERRAN TRINIDAD
OSTEOPATIA
FERRAN@COTG-OSTEOPATIA.COM

ISABEL TRINIDAD
MÈTODE FELDENKRAIS
REEDUCACIÓ POSTURAL GLOBAL
MÒBIL 653 467 745
ISABEL@COTG-OSTEOPATIA.COM

PARQUE DA CIDADE

Parque da Cidade (City Park)

Designer Marta Afonso

This project is a mapping exercise reflecting the chromatic variation of the flora found along a walking trail in Oporto City Park. The process began with the collection of samples from leaves of all tree species and the registration of its predominant color as well as the location of all individuals of the same species. The information gathered in a sort of herbarium was then related to the geographical frequency of each species resulting in a publication and an infographic.

Flip book calendar, Youth service Kranj

Designer Tomato Košir Copywriter Tomato Košir, Teja Kleč Client Youth service Kranj

A student calendar that starts in the fall and ends in the summer. The deciduous tree is a metaphor for student work — it starts as a tabula rasa, then gains leaves during the learning process, and at the end of the year the fruits of students' work are harvested.

Lufhereng

Design Agency Grid Worldwide Branding and Design Designer Marette Koortz Client Gauteng Housing and City of Joburg

"Lufhereng" is derived from both a Tshivenda word and Sotho word — "Lufhera" and "reng" respectively. The combined word refers to a place where people come together with a unified commitment. The Lufhereng project is also planned to include all other land uses normally associated with a sustainable urban development: social, institutional, commercial, municipal and public open space. Its goal is the development of sustainable human settlements over the next five years, and the creation of a space which will facilitate the development of a community where people value each other and work together to achieve a better quality of life. The identity tries to embrace and communicate the growth, potential, natural integration and connection of this project.

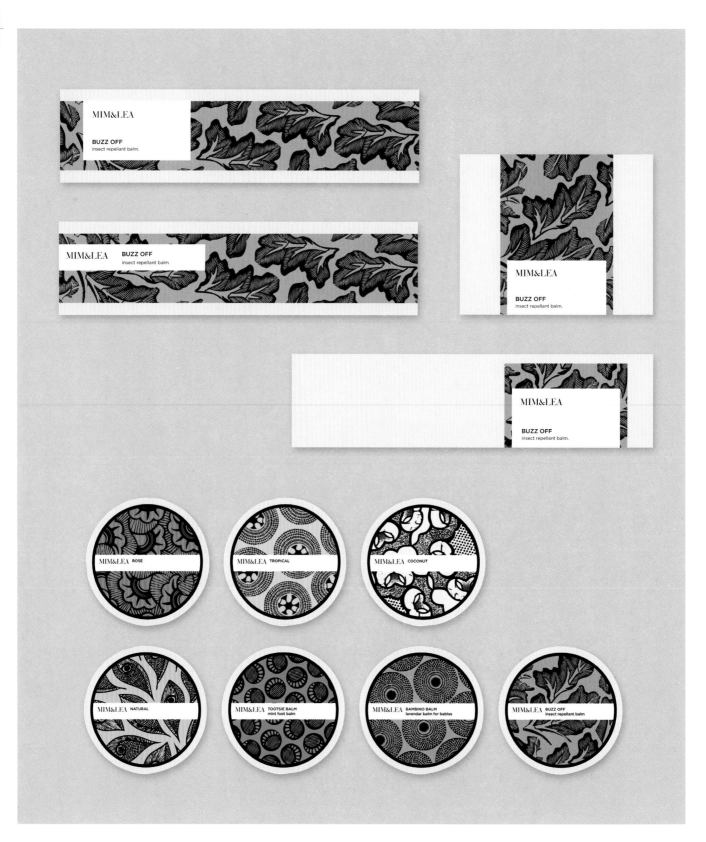

Mim & Lea

Design Agency Hardhat Design Designer Jenny Miles, Nickolus Clifford Client Mim & Lea

Based in Australia and Accra (Ghana), Mim & Lea is a fashion and lifestyle company producing and selling luxury clothing, interiors and beauty products with an African feel. The project seen here included brand creation, development of the company logo, and application of both across packaging and labels (primarily their beauty range of body balms and scented candles). The brand and packaging needed to reflect a mix of both modern luxury and traditional African design. This was achieved using a combination of modern western fonts and clean minimal layout alongside bold colours and traditional African prints which reference the plant-based ingredients in their products.

BEE REFRESHED
Peppermint

BEE ENERGISED
Lime, Grapefruit & Chamomile

BEE SEXY
Rose Geranium

BEE ZEN
Lavender

BUZZ OFF
Lemongrass & Citronella

MIM&LEA

MIM&LEA

MIM&LEA

MIM&LEA

MIM&LEA

BEE REFRESHED
Peppermint

MIM&LEA

BEE ENERGISED
Lime, Grapefruit & Chamomile

MIM&LEA

BEE SEXY
Rose Geranium

MIM&LEA

BEE ZEN
Lavender

MIM&LEA

MIM&LEA
BEE REFRESHED
Peppermint

MIM&LEA
BEE ENERGISED
Lime, Grapefruit & Chamomile

MIM&LEA
BEE SEXY
Rose Geranium

MIM&LEA
BEE ZEN
Lavender

MIM&LEA
BUZZ OFF
Lemongrass & Citronella

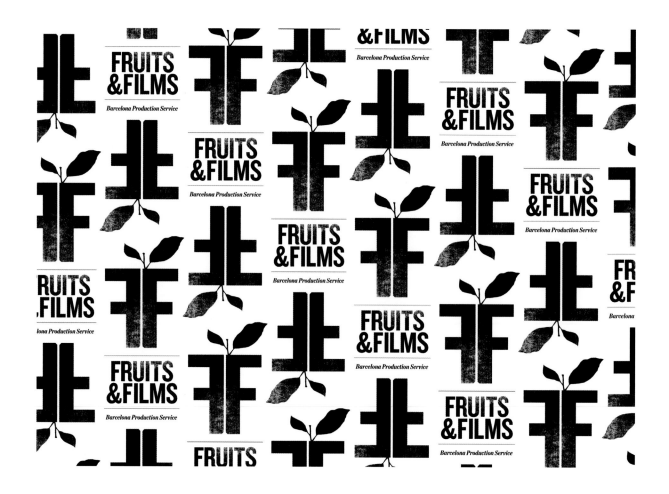

EVA BERGMAN
Production

Paseo de la Barceloneta 32, IA
Barcelona 08024
P+34 934 238 556
F+34 934 238 556
eva@fruitsandfilms.com
www.fruitsandfilms.com

Fruits & Films

Design Agency Lo Siento Creative Director Borja Martinez Client FRUITS & FILMS
Production Service Company in Barcelona.

Nayara Rampazzo Business Card

Designer Lucas Rampazzo Client Nayara Rampazzo (Nutritionist)

A series of business cards for a nutritionist using illustrations of healthy foods.

the FIRST EDITION
of
MY HAND DRAWN
[FIELD] STUDY INSPIRED

ILLUSTRATED
and DESIGNED
by SASHA PROOD

Field Study Inspired Poster & Card

Designer Sasha Prood

Sasha Prood's goal of transforming vintage field illustrations into unique letterforms became a detailed study of nature and an example of her true aesthetic. As a starting point for the project, she researched plant and fungi types to inspire an authentic visual variety. As she began drawing the letters, she carefully analyzed which plant or fungi would fit each letter in an effortless, organic way. As in her previous works, in this project she was striving for an organic style of illustration.

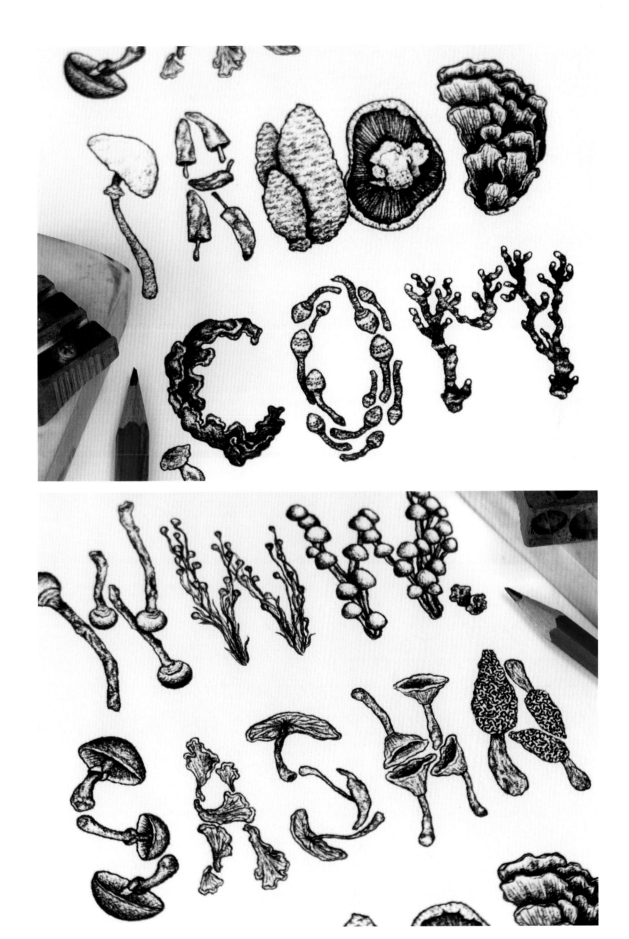

Vila Florida

Design Agency Lo Siento Creative Director Borja Martinez Client Anna & Pitu

This bar and restaurant is set inside a civic center with a garden, so the whole identity represents that atmosphere. With the botanical elements and a bright green as the only color, the result feels fresh and natural.

Merindades. Gusto Navarro

<u>Design Agency</u> Comuniza <u>Designer</u> Olga Llopis <u>Illustrator</u> Eduardo Valero <u>Copywriter</u> Javier Velilla <u>Client</u> Merindades

This visual identity was conceived for a retail location specializing in handcrafted products with Navarre Designation of Origin. The brand concept is based on core values such as quality, authenticity, and honesty. The messages and illustrations traced by pencil on paper relate to the handcrafted goods. They also invite people to adopt a healthy diet by eating wholesome slow food.

MERINDADES
GUSTO NAVARRO

La flor con el corazón más tierno

Muy pronto estaremos a tu servicio
Teléfono 937 961 477 / www.merindadesdenavarra.es

MERINDADES
GUSTO NAVARRO

Rico, rico, gusto navarrico

Muy pronto estaremos a tu servicio
Teléfono 937 961 477 / www.merindadesdenavarra.es

Berlin Paper Company Paper Promotion

Designer Laura J. Merriman

This project was about creating a unique paper promotion that showcased characteristics of different paper samples. Laura wanted to create a piece that promoted recycled papers and supported the movement to save forests. Printing bark textures on the back of each sample showcases the beauty of each tree and useful plant information allows the user to learn about the plant that produces paper. This group of samples allows the viewer to understand the qualities of recycled paper and also gain an appreciation for the plants that provide it. Learning about the environment is one step toward supporting its survival.

County Line Harvest Branding & Farm Boxes

Design Agency Shegeek Design/Seed Designer Brett Walkley, Mary Kate Meyerhoffer Illustrator Jane Kim Photographer Al Liu
Client County Line Harvest

One of the most highly regarded farms in Northern California, Petaluma-based County Line Harvest is an organic farm known for their specialty baby lettuces. These signature lettuces are served at acclaimed restaurants from San Francisco to Los Angeles. Last year the farm opened a new growing facility just outside of Palm Springs in Southern California.

With its business growing and two outposts, County Line Harvest needed two different logos (one for each farm) that would create a strong visual bond. Small farms, such as County Line Harvest, have traditionally used a middleman to distribute their produce but are increasingly realizing that a strong brand can help increase brand loyalty and boost direct sales. With this in mind, Shegeek Design/Seed created a strong and bold branding system that worked to tie both farms together. This system included a logo for each farm, farm boxes, print and interactive design, and a logo for County Line's Rogue Markets, which are pop-up farmers' markets outside of top San Francisco restaurants.

Urban Seed

Designer Caroline Morris

Urban Seed is a non-profit organization that exists to inspire a new generation of people to build relationships with healthy food, farming, and the land. Through educational development programs, Urban Seed provides an outlet for community enrichment while supplying fresh, local produce. The organization is located on Dudley Farm in Nashville, TN.

The 5th annual Field-to-Fork benefit dinner serves to promote the ideals of Urban Seed. The purpose of the dinner is to raise awareness and funding for the organization while giving participants a genuine dining experience. The event is located on the farm itself, bringing people directly to the source of their food. Participants should leave with a better understanding of Urban Seed and feel motivated to support the organization financially. Deliverables for the farm, organization, and benefit dinner all needed to perform in a cohesive manner. Inspired by a utilitarian mindset, black ink was chosen to aid in this cohesion while being budget conscious. The monochromatic paper selection also created harmony for the project.

Chiswick

Design Agency Frost Designer Vince Frost Photographer Dieu Tan Client Morsul

Frost's brief was to create a brand that would position Matt Moran's new restaurant, Chiswick, as a relaxed neighborhood diner nestled in a unique, historic garden setting. The collateral includes all customer facing and corporate applications: signage, website, menu, wine list, uniforms, bill presenters, canvas tote bags, tea towels, coasters and stationery. Frost's creative solution was inspired by the site's historic gardens, and the recently planted 150 square metre vegetable garden that will supply the restaurant with fresh produce. Every element of the design has a botanical influence — from the logo design featuring tendril-like typography, through to the soft muted palette, sustainable materials and photographic studies of plants drawn from the gardens. The solution is elegant, sensual and totally grounded in an appreciation of the natural elements that make the restaurant such a special place.

Arantza Loradenda

Design Agency Mai Design Designer Maite Elias Uria Client Arantza Loradenda

Arantza is a florist that has been located in Zarautz (Spain) since 1986. Last year, the entire identity was reinvented – the shop design, branding, interior decoration, and services were all improved. In order to create a new atmosphere, the florist covered the walls with black and white flower details to give the branding harmony and draw attention to the colors of the living flowers in the shop. The visual inspiration came from exploring industry magazines and websites.

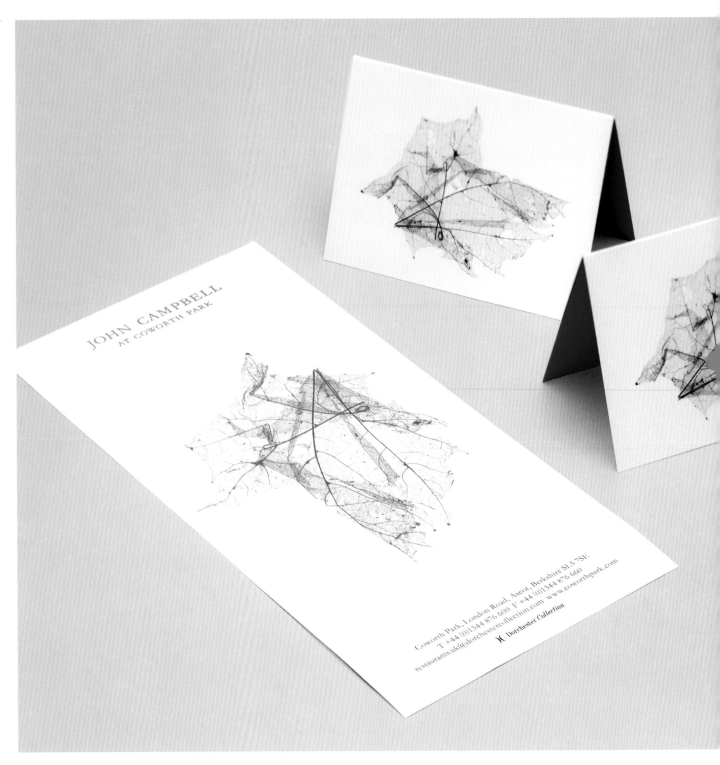

John Campbell at Coworth Park

Design Agency & SMITH Photographer Giles Revell Client Coworth Park

The fine dining offer at Dorchester Collection's 5 star country retreat, John Campbell at Coworth Park, serves an innovative British menu courtesy of the acclaimed chef. To distinguish the restaurant while complementing Coworth Park's look and feel, the identity suggests a refined tone appropriate to the restaurant's food and interiors. Led by an elegant logotype, ephemeral images of leaves (by photographer Giles Revell), and natural colours with copper accents, the identity hints at the surrounding countryside while suggesting the seasonal ingredients and intricate methods employed in John Campbell's cooking.

Holly BURGER
DONOSTIA ‡ SAN SEBASTIÁN

SOME HOLLY BURGERS ‡

HEAVEN CAN WAIT
Puré de patatas,
cebolla confitada .... **6,5€**
PROVENCE PRO
Mermelada de cebolla,
queso brie .... **7€**
RICHELIEU
Queso roquefort,
pera caramelizada .... **7,5€**
PASSION RED
Pimientos orgánicos .... **6,5€**
STREETS OF PHILADELPHIA
Queso philadelphia,
cebolla confitada, nueces .... **7€**

TU NUEVA HAMBURGUESERÍA EN SAN SEBASTIÁN!

FOLLOW US ON
facebook

Holly Burger, Calle Pescadería 6
Donostia, 943423759

Holly BURGER
DONOSTIA ‡ SAN SEBASTIÁN

‡ **WISH LIST** ‡
C.Pescadería 6, Donostia, San Sebastián

HOLLY HAMBURGERS ‡

HEAVEN CAN WAIT
Mashed potatoes,
confit onion .... 6,5€
PROVENCE PRO
Onion marmalade,
brie cheese .... 7€
RICHELIEU
Roquefort cheese,
confit pear .... 7,5€
PASSION RED
Organic peppers .... 6,5€

LE CLASSIC
Lettuce, onion, tomato, pickles 5,5€
LE CLASSIC SAY CHEESE
Lettuce, onion, tomato,
pickles, cheese .... 6€
LE CLASSIC SAY CHEESE & BACON
Lettuce, tomato, pickles,
onion, cheese, bacon .... 6,5€
STREETS OF PHILADELPHIA
Philadelpia cheese,
confit onion, walnuts .... 7€

HOLLY SANDWHICHES ‡

VEGGIEWOOD
Tomato, lettuce,
onion, mayo .... 5€
CLUB SANDWICH
Chicken, bacon, tomato,
lettuce, onion, mayo .... 5,5€
MADRAS CLUB
Curry chicken, tomato,
lettuce, red onion .... 6€

TERIYAKI CLUB
Teriyaki chicken, tomato,
lettuce, red onion .... 5,5€
HOLLY SANDWICH
Chicken, confit onion,
egg, lettuce .... 5,5€
MON BIKINI
Ham, cheese .... 5€

HOLLY STARTERS ‡

CONVENT CHICKEN WINGS 4,5€
ONION RINGS OF FIRE .... 4€
CAESAR'S SALAD .... 6,5€
TRINITY CHEESE SALAD 6,5€
DIVINE FRENCH FRIES .... 3€

HOLLY DESSERTS ‡

CHOCOLATE TRINITY
Three textures of chocolate ... 4€
HOLLY CHEESECAKE
From New York to Heaven ...... 4€
HOLLY ICE CREAMS
Cool your passions .... 3,5€

FOLLOW US ON
facebook

‡ **ENGLISH** ‡
T 94 342 37 59

HOLLY BURGER

Design Agency Rodrigo Aguadé Studio **Graphic Designer** Manuel Astorga, Rodrigo Aguadé **Client** HOLLY BURGER

Holly Burger is the coolest new burger restaurant in San Sebastián in Spain. The restaurant is named after Holly, the aunt of the restaurant owner, Iñigo Otegui. She is the one responsible for many of the secret burger recipes offered on their delicious menu. Rodrigo Aguadé Studio's idea was to create a real American-style brand with a fresh mix of style references. Their inspiration came from various vintage, hand-drawn American typographies present in old shop windows and banana leaf wallpaper that had been originally designed in 1942 by decorator Don Loper for the Beverly Hills hotel in Los Angeles, California.

Las verduras de muchas maneras

Design Agency Mot Designer Laia Clos Illustrator Juliet Pomés Client Zahorí

A vegetables cookbook with over 1,200 recipes prepared in many different ways, as well as promotional material for the book: a calendar, a poster, a set of postcards, and bookmarks.

Biodiversity Protection

Design Agency Principle Design Designer Sash Fernando, Anthony Fernando Photographer Ross Campbell Client Biodiversity Protection Inc.

Biodiversity Protection Inc. is a group of fundraising organizations that works to protect the environment, at a state level across Australia and internationally. They also assist in fund generation for local charities that support environmental sustainability. The identity system unifies the group's various regional offices with a common visual language, yet imbues each with a distinctly individual persona. Using "branch" in both its figurative and literal sense, the design for each element emanates from a tree native to the relevant geographic locality.

Delish Café Concept Identity

Design Agency Nae-Design Designer Dr. Nae West

Gourmet sandwich company Delish required a fresh identity to complement their organic menu selections and differentiate their business from competitors. To emphasize Delish's natural ingredients and the marketing themes of "science", "wholesome" and "simple", Dr. Nae West drew inspiration from her scientific background and researched creative styles of botanical illustration. The result is a classically styled hand-drawn logo and packaging that accentuates healthiness and well-being, whilst paying homage to chef-crafted delicacies.

Dell' Albero Limoncello

Design Agency Boldincreative Pty Ltd Creative Director Jon Clark Design Directors Kent Walker, Jarrod Robertson Designer Luca Uboldi Finished Artist Matt Morris Copywriter Andrew Georgiou, Copy&Co. Photographer Ico Hernandez Client Ambra Limoncello

A traditional Italian liqueur, Limoncello has long been crafted from secretly guarded family recipes handed down through generations. This history introduced us to the Dell' Albero way of handcrafting Limoncello — from the very finest lemons. The fact that the name Dell' Albero translates to 'from the tree' seemed fitting and seamlessly validated our choice. Inspiration for the packaging design was derived from the very orchards that bear the lemons used to make this unique liqueur. By way of tradition, the base of each lemon tree is coated with white paint to deter crawling insects from reaching the fruit.

A slender, frosted flint bottle displays the vibrant hue of the Limoncello and is finished with the same handcrafted quality as the liqueur itself. White packaging twine (similar to that used to bundle harvested lemons), coils around the sleek neck where three labels rest. The labels act as glimpses into the story and tradition behind Dell' Albero Limoncello and are debossed in two colours printed on natural cotton stock using traditional Letterpress techniques. The bottle is hand-finished with white sealing wax to complete this refreshing offer. A white ceramic base resembling the tree trunk is an integral part of the design and provides a functional purpose by acting as both a stand and 'chiller' for the bottle when placed in the freezer prior to serving. Two ceramic shot glasses accompany the cooler base and are shaped as the nodes of a tree branch. These can also be stored in the freezer for an icy cold nip.

Dell'Albero

LIMONCELLO

IT BEGINS WITH A SECRET,
KNOWN ONLY TO FAMILY,
SHAPED BY TRADITION,
GENERATIONALLY SHARED.
CREATED WITH THE HAND,
CRAFTED FROM THE HEART,
THIS AGE-OLD CUSTOM,
FINDS LIFE 'FROM THE TREE'.

Moya

Designer Daniel Berkowitz

Moya is a range of high-end spa products produced solely from South African Fynbos and sold locally and abroad. The use of simple raw materials, austere design and high-end production techniques gives Moya a sophisticated look that has an African feel delivered in an international way.

SNOWBU...

...ephalus africand...
...aromatic
...emary look-
...ke has been
...aditionally used
...in remedies
...since the days
of the first
settlers, around
1677. Anecdotally
known for its mood
enhancing and sedative
qualities, the Cape
Snowbush has a proud
history in the South
African home, finding use as
a natural hair tonic,
decongestant, cold & flu reliever
and has even proven effective in
the easing and relaxation of
muscular pains.

...cinal
...and other
...als in a range
...necare
...d from the finest
...and essential oils
...the energy, vitality
...l goodness of Africa
...est form.

CAPE GERANIUM
(Pelargoneum
graveolens)
In times gone by, the
fragrant deep-green
oil extracted from
this endemic plant
found use in a great
variety of remedies
and was even
applied in treating
fractures. Recently, the
Geranium has become
appreciated for its balancing
and tonic like effect on the Liver
and Kidneys and has proven to
be effective in detoxifying the
system, assisting in weight loss
and in treating cellulite - while
calming and assuaging the mind.

...peopl...
Besides its
calming,
uplifting and
thought focusing
properties, Buchu is
useful in treating
arthritis,
rheumatism, kidney
and urinary infections.
In more modern times,
Buchu's uses have extended
into the treatment of water
retention and cellulite.

CAPE MAY (Coleonema album)
Praised for its beautiful shower
of blooms, this species of
Fynbos has been found
in South African
gardens for
generations, where
many of its practical
implications
have been
discovered.
Campers,
fishermen
and chefs have
used Cape May as
a natural insect
repellent and odour
neutraliser, but the
extracts are known to relax and
soothe the mind. The plant's
gentle medicinal properties are
used in relieving fevers, sore
throats, aches & pains.

...house...
Zinziba has...
used in treating
asthma, bronchitis,
fevers, and in aiding
recovery after illness.
As a natural emollient,
Zinziba creams and
essential oils soothe and
nourish irritated skin.

LANYANA (Artemisia afra)
Lanyana (or African Wormwood)
is indigenous to the mountainous
regions of South Africa. Used
in rituals by native tribes for
narcotic purposes, small
doses of Lanyan...
extract hold
excellent m...
qualities...
teas al...
stom...
diso...
vap...
bo...
e...
ailm...

...the Ca...
...been
...clea...
...Af...
...c...

also treats h...
symptoms,
as a mild
skin abr...

Eibel and Glow Brand Identity

Designer Oriol Gil Client Eibel and Glow

Eibel and Glow is a small perfume shop in Barcelona that creates perfumes for its customers. Based on four basic essences, a perfume designer creates a personalized fragrance. The project required the design of the entire brand, logo, and stationery materials. The French village of Grasse, the world center of perfume since the end of the 18th century, was the inspiration for the logotype and graphics. The trays, test tubes and the perfume designer's materials, their signs, numbers and graphic universe all were designed cohesively. The palette of materials, colors and styles were inspired by the photography of Ikebana compositions of 1970s Japanese books. Wood, papyrus, glass, and plants resulted in an ikebana laboratory.

Naturligtvis Identity and Product Line

Designer Saga Mariah Sandberg Copywriter Arvid Ringborg Photographer Ztefan Bertha Client Naturligtvis

Naturligtvis is a range of organic, locally produced skin care products with a unisex profile. The design is made with a focus on relaxed simplicity to appeal to a broad range of consumers as well as communicating the pure and natural content. The name of the brand "Naturligtvis" has three meanings in Swedish. The first is "naturally" (without a doubt), the second is "in a natural manner," and the third is "naturally wise."

To keep the simplicity of the design, yet communicate the humorous and warm personality of the brand, each product has a clever story printed on the packaging. Through these labels, the customer can learn fun and interesting facts about the key ingredients of the product.

SALVIDERM

NATURLIGT VIS

Shampoo
kelp
30 ml

SALVIDERM

NATURLIGT VIS

Hand Cream
marigold
30 ml

SALVIDERM

NATURLIGT VIS

Shower Gel
blood orange
30 ml

SALVIDERM

NATURLI
VIS

Body Lo
palmaro
30 ml

Kotoha with yuica

Design Agency T-Square Design Associates Designer Eiji Tsuda Client Sei-Plus Co.

T-Square Design Associates developed an entirely new line of toiletry products containing "yuica" — pure essential oils extracted from a wide variety of trees in Japan. They developed all aspects of the brand from positioning, naming, and packaging to communication tools. The concept embodies the brand essence, which is to refresh and regain Japanese senses, and to artistically capture the essence of pure nature. Designers used the motif of a drop coming out of a leaf as the key visual in developing the logo to express the concept of yuica, which is the essence of Japanese forests distilled into concentrated oils.

The name, KOTOHA, comes from the words "trees and leaves" as well as the linguistic root of the Japanese expression for "words" (kotoba), which includes "leaves" because they represent richness in nature. For the packaging, high quality paper boxes are chosen to encase the bottles so that the first interaction people have with the products is with a material that comes from nature. The color schemes used for the two scents represent the relative therapeutic effects of their aromas: orange for Nioikobushi, which has energizing effects, and green for Kuromoji, which has calming effects.

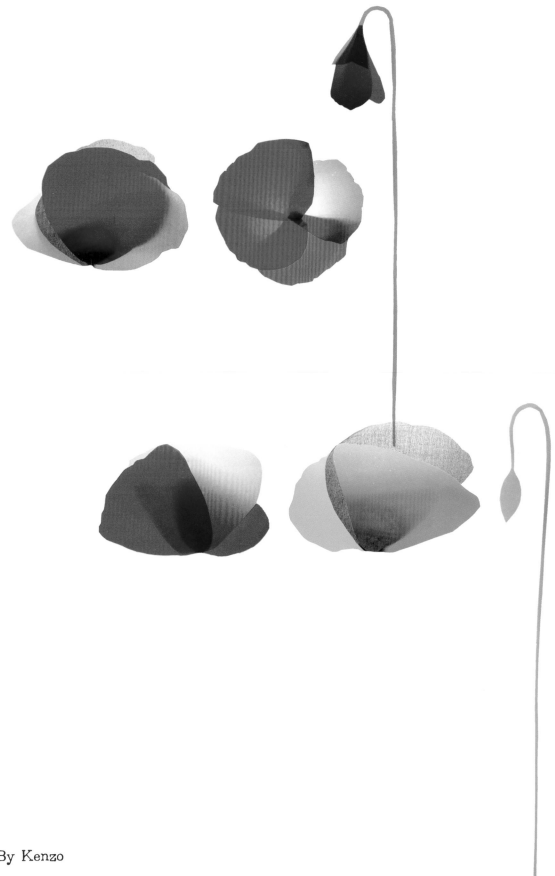

Flower By Kenzo

Designer Zaijia Huang

Over the past few years, Zaijia has made several designs for the Kenzo perfume. From the flowered gift packaging to the perfume bottle and a series of festival gift packages, Kenzo designed every detail as part of a larger artistic picture.

Flower by Kenzo is a household name; this project was for the 2011 summer limited edition. Zaijia cut out the shape of petals with a scissor, and gave them unrealistic color: red, blue and fuchsia. The poppy created a brand new image hanging from a sky-blue branch. Zaijia also illustrated a city which perfectly matched this imaginary flower.

KENZO

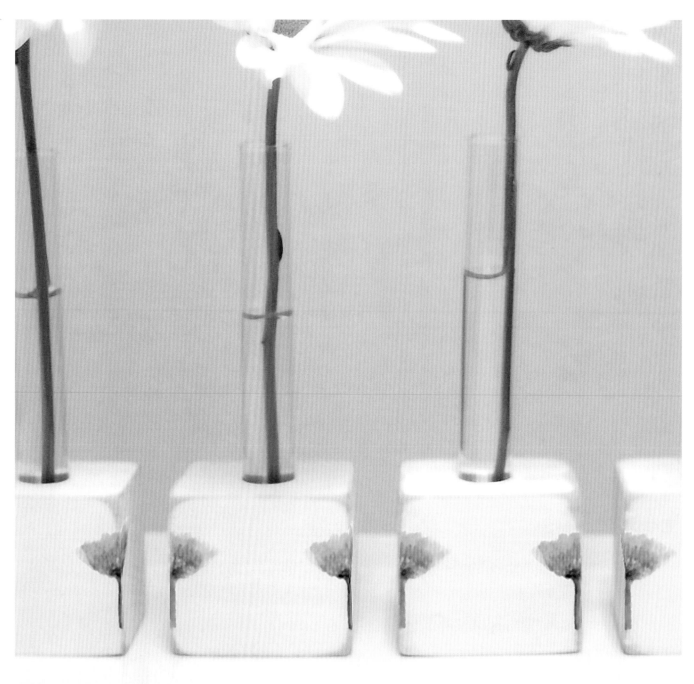

BLOSSOM

Designer Nuri Cha

The word "Blossom" often inspires people to imagine Spring. When Spring comes, flowers bloom and people feel warmth. Designer Nuri Cha graphically represented the promise of Spring through a sumi style flower.

BLOSSOM

BLOSSOM

Garden Lighting
Company

Garden Lighting Company

Design Agency The Chase Client Garden Lighting Company

The Garden Lighting Company designs and installs contemporary lighting solutions that allow people to appreciate and enjoy their gardens in the evenings as much as they do during the day. The logo uses flowers in the form of lampshades to link the company inextricably with its core offer.

Naturopathica Rebranding

<u>Design Agency</u> Elixir Design <u>Creative Director</u> Jennifer Jerde <u>Designer</u> Scott Hesselink <u>Photographer</u> University and Jepson Herbaria <u>Client</u> Naturopathica

Naturopathica, founded in 1995 and based in East Hampton, New York, reached out to Elixir for a rebranding to go along with the relaunch of a skin and beauty line. At that time, the line was carried by select high profile spas around the country and sold direct online. Naturopathica enjoyed a small loyal following but was frustrated by a fiercely competitive marketplace brimming with false claims. Barbara Close, Founder and CEO, knew the brand was flying under the radar and suspected that the packaging's home-grown look and misperceptions about the performance of botanical skin care were factors that needed to be addressed.

Elixir conducted interviews with current & prospective customers and spa partners to help Naturopathica understand how their brand was perceived. The findings illuminated the gap between current perceptions and desired positioning, inspiring the company to undertake a comprehensive retooling of everything from product to packaging. The company reformulated many of its products and included many sustainable, certified organic, and herbal ingredients to earn ECOCERT certification. Elixir developed an elevator pitch and redesign of Naturopathica brand's visual language, including identity, business system, style guide, and packaging for nearly 100 products. The cohesive system integrated images of herbarium specimens, obtained from the University and Jepson Herbaria at UC Berkeley, which houses two voluminous collections of pressed plants.

NATUROPATHICA®

July 11, 2007

Nathaniel Hawthorne
Community Activist
Brook Farm
27 Hardy Street
Salem, MA 01970

Dear Mr. Hawthorne,

It's not often, sir, that one chances upon your name during casual conversation. I was at my
favorite local bookstore the other day when the cashier, who also happens to be the owner,
up a few words with me. He noticed that I had placed two books on the countertop, both by
American contemporary writers.

"Did you know that today is Nathaniel Hawthorne's birthday?" he opened knowingly. "It w
the AM talk station that discusses literature for reading geeks. The announcer said that Nat
Hawthorne was the first great American novelist."

"I'm not sure I agree with you on that one," I good-naturedly responded to the cashier.

"Well," he quipped, as he placed my purchases into a brown bag. "Think of it this way: The
of American literature is fairly new and young compared its counterparts. Remember, peop
had not been composing extensive literary pieces in this country for that long. Hawthorne
milestone."

I know it seems a bit petty but something about the cashier's words actually stayed with m
day. It wasn't until I had finished brushing my teeth that night that I realized why I interna
voiced such dissent at his thoughts.

I know this letter has been nothing short of long-winded, Mr. Hawthorne, but the epiphan
to my story is the point behind why I am writing you. Sir, while you may have been one of
whirlwind firsts, I don't consider all frontrunners in the same realm of deserving greatness
you were monumental in your achievement, but I feel you were far too concerned with he
handed Debbie Downer Puritanical metaphors in your writing. Your overuse of allegory w
definitely on the borderline of pastiche.

Sincerely,

A Very Concerned Fan of Literature

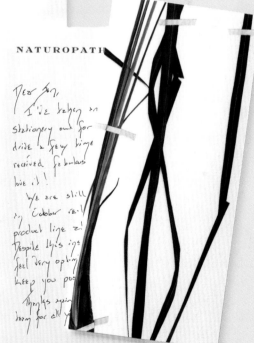

Sic Herb Kit

Designer Donna Cheng

Sic Herb Kit is a medicinal herbal starter kit that includes all the essentials for a beginner to start planting their own herbs with clear instructions. Each kit includes seeds, identification cards, a water atomizer, plant food, a shovel, storage for dried leaves and roots, and an instructional guide. The guide is an infographic displaying the method of how and when to properly harvest the twelve selected medicinal herbs. The guidelines are implemented on the timeline shown at the bottom of each page to reference when the herbs are in season during the span of the calendar year. There are also twelve icons to give a visual illustration of how deep and wide to plant the herbs, and the important parts of each herb that contain medicinal benefits are also marked. The information is shown in a scientific yet reader friendly way to guide the audience into taking on the task of creating a healthy and eco friendly environment.

The name "sic" came from its definition and its sound resemblance to "sick", which is a playful name for a medicinal herbal kit. The definition of sic references a passage that was intentionally written and set exactly as found in the original source, the "root". The metaphor of this word led to its brand name and logo, which is a root symbol.

Victory Garden NYC

Design Agency Paperwhite Studio Photographer Zandy Magold Client Victory Garden NYC

Victory Garden in New York's West Village offers local goat milk ice cream, flavored with essences from the Middle East. Goat milk has a delicious slightly sweet flavor, as well as a lot of nutritional benefits. Paperwhite Studio created an identity to reflect the fresh farm nature of the ice cream.

Victory Garden – New York City

http://victorygardennyc.com/wp/

Apple Yahoo! Google Maps YouTube Wikipedia News (138) ▾ Popular ▾

VICTORY
GARDEN
new york city

About   Contact   Blog   twitter   facebook

— Spring toppings —

· Strawberries ·   · Stewed Rhubarb ·

— from the Blog —

Hand Embroidered Lavender Sachets
Goods and Goodies | posted on 8/5/10

I adore these sachets. They are embroidered by hand with floral motifs and filled with high quality dried lavender from Provence. I love how detailed and delicate they are, and how they bring back the quality of handmade gifts from times past. These make beautiful gifts for baby showers, bridal showers, weddings, and hostess gifts. Place ...

read more »

— Spring flavors —

· Neroli Vanilla ·
with Tahitian Vanilla beans

· Lavender ·

· Damascene Rose & Mastic ·

— Spring Sundaes —

ETHIOPIAN COFFEE
WITH CARDAMOM

winter

TURKISH DELIGHT

Damascene Rose with Mastic

spring

BASIL & MINT

summer

DARK CHOCOLATE
ROSEMARY

autumn

MOREL

Designer Zaijia Huang Client MOREL

This is a personal logo and CD design for musician MOREL.

MOREL

Rebranding for woodberry's

Design Agency asatte design office Designer Satoshi Kondo Illustrator Tomoaki Kamei Client woodberry's Ltd.

This is a rebranding for the frozen yogurt shop "woodberry's", which makes frozen yogurt with homemade yogurt and fresh fruit from farmers. Designer Satoshi Kondo focused on the pureness of the materials and their fresh taste, since woodberry's doesn't use any preservatives or a heating process. It feels like the fresh ingredients are absorbed into the body like water.

This is the strongest point of their product so Satoshi Kondo used watercolor paintings for their visual communication. Watercolor permeates into white paper beautifully. The white paper clearly expresses the freshness and coolness of woodberry's frozen yogurt, so Satoshi Kondo used it for the shop card and menu card as well. The symbol of two drops means receiving a blessing from nature and passing that blessing onto customers.

ウッドベリーズ
生フローズンヨーグルト
吉祥寺
http://woodberrys.co.jp
1
Point Card

ウッドベリーズ
生フローズンヨーグルト
吉祥寺
http://woodberrys.co.jp
2
Point Card

ウッドベリーズ
生フローズンヨーグルト
吉祥寺
http://woodberrys.co.jp
3
Point Card

ウッドベリーズ
生フローズンヨーグルト
吉祥寺
http://woodberrys.co.jp
4
Point Card

ウッドベリーズ
生フローズンヨーグルト
吉祥寺
http://woodberrys.co.jp
5
Point Card

ウッドベリーズ
生フローズンヨーグルト
吉祥寺
http://woodberrys.co.jp
6
Point Card

Tea & Sympathy

Designer Andrea Ataz

This is the package design for a fruit and herbal tea company. Andrea Ataz designed an icon for each fruit: lemon, grape, orange, strawberry and apple. Each pack corresponds to a different flavor and contains the tea bags. Andrea Ataz also designed a promotional pack, which contains a tea bag of each flavor and samples of grape tea.

tea and sympathy.

5 bolsitas
Peso neto 8g

Disfruta tu momento simpático del día
con nuestra gama de tés. Todos están
elaborados a partir de frutas 100%
naturales. Tu sólo tendrás que añadir
agua calentita y a disfrutar.

Puedes elegir entre cinco sabores de té:
limón, naranja, fresa, uva y manzana.
Todos ellos con el toque especial
simpático que los hace diferentes.

Flowergala

Design Agency BLOW Designer Ken Lo, Crystal Cheung, Caspar Ip Client Polytrade Paper Corporation Limited

Over the past 35 years, Polytrade Paper Corporation has been introducing different overseas paper brands and innovative paper uses into the market. This time, Polytrade has brought to BLOW the Astrobrights papers that come in 23 bright colors that get people's attention. To launch this new paper series, Polytrade held a launch party at a restaurant in Macau. BLOW was asked to create the event name, identity, promotional materials and decor for the event.

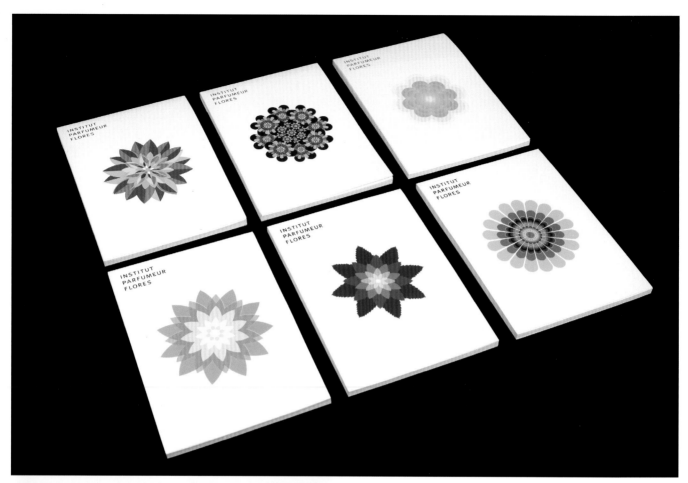

Institut Parfumeur Flores

Design Agency Bunch

This project is the identity and branding design for the Zagreb perfumery the Institut Parfumeur Flores. A pallet of many colored flowers was created for the brand to keep it sweetly playful and diverse. The branding includes signage, bags, stickers, pencils, ribbons and labels along with various promotional applications that were applied to both the interior and exterior of the store.

WITH COMPLIMENTS

INSTITUT
PARFUMEUR
FLORES

DEŽMANOV PROLAZ
10000 ZAGREB
T +385 1 4
F +385
WW

INSTITUT PARFUMEUR FLORES

Green LAB Identity

Designer Diana Gibadulina Illustrator Katya Berezina Photographer Adam Mørk

Green LAB is a restaurant, laboratory, and shop. Vegetables, fruits, and herbs are grown at the restaurant and customers can choose the ingredients for their dish themselves. The identity is based on green dots symbolizing order and ingredients for the meal. Each dot is unique and an irregular shape shows that they are natural, not man made. When you buy something at the shop your bag or box is tagged with a label on which your purchase is marked with a sticker. The menu is interactive: customers drag their favorite ingredients onto their plate and the system generates a selection of menu items using those ingredients for them to choose from.

Oxygen in the park

Designer Federica Marziale Photographer David Beltran

A walk in the warm sun and flowers blooming — this was the moment when the idea of "Oxygen in the park" came into being. The project's primary aim is a return to nature. "Oxygen in the park" wants to attract people to the park every Sunday and invite them to live in contact with nature through healthy activities like yoga, good music, picnics, and sports. Behind this idea is the belief in freedom and respect for nature. The poetic vision for the project is picking mushrooms in the woods, eating flowers, and falling in love with nature.

Mori Chiropractic Clinic

Design Agency E. Co., Ltd. Designer Kenichi Matsumoto Copywriter Kensaku Kamada

The concept for the clinic is that it should be a place that both provides chiropractic treatment and is an enjoyable place for having a cup of tea over a leisurely chat. Mori means "forest" in English. Fingerprints are used to convey the forest trees and also the concept of all people from young to old gathering here, and finding relief through healing hands. The characters were formed with gaps between the strokes to represent the space found between bones by the chiropractor's fingers. There are variations on the logo that represent the four different seasons as experienced in Japan.

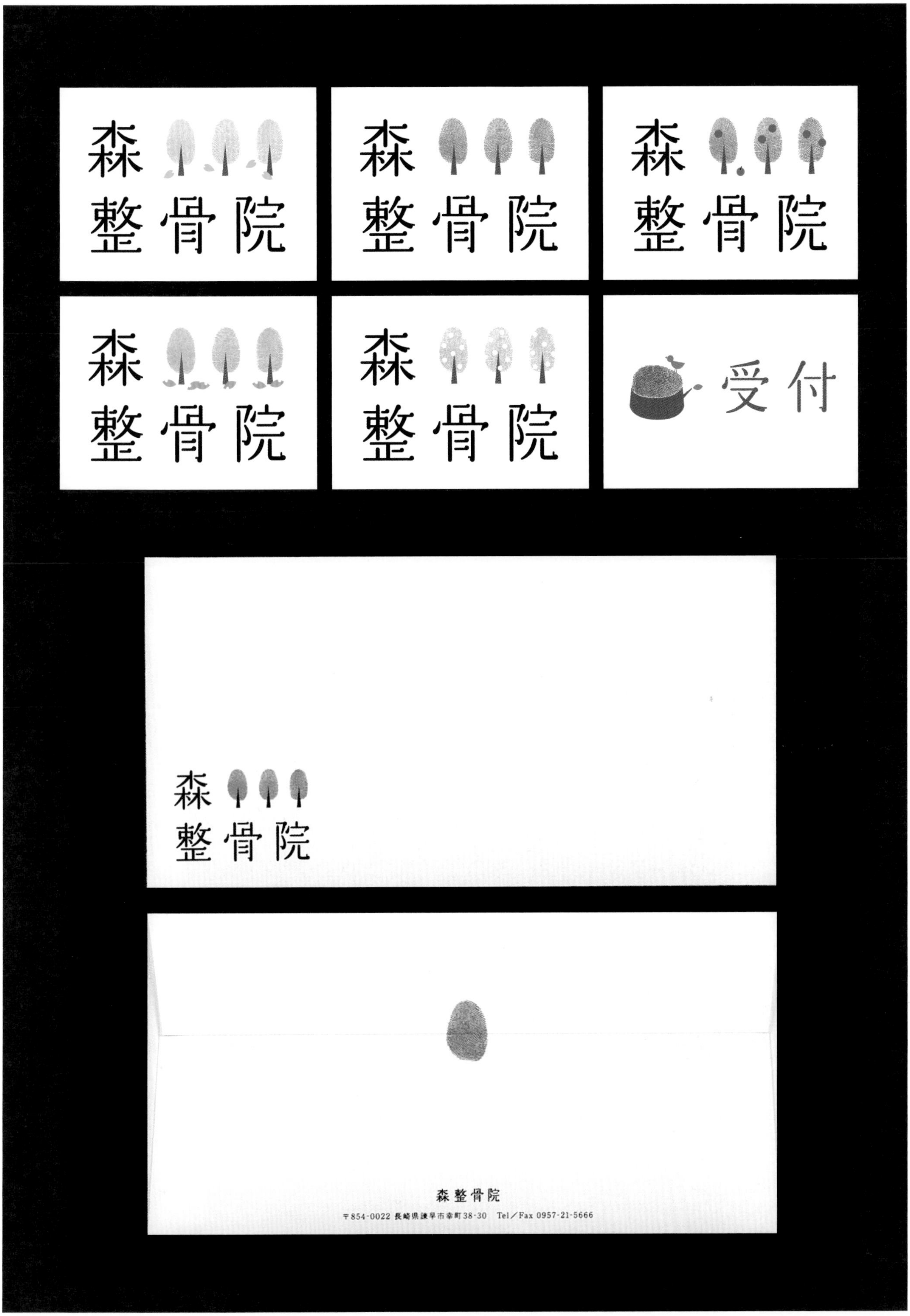

森整骨院

森整骨院

森整骨院

森整骨院

森整骨院

受付

森整骨院

森整骨院
〒854-0022 長崎県諫早市幸町38-30　Tel／Fax 0957-21-5666

More Trees Exhibition - Feeling the Forest for 12 days

Design Agency Nakano Design Office Co., Ltd. Designer Takeo Nakano Copywriter Ako Sugie Photographer Takumi Ota Client more trees, AXIS GALLERY

This is the graphic design for the "More Trees" exhibition put together by the forest preservation organization. The poster was designed as if the building was one big tree. For the graphic panel at the exhibition site, Nakano Design Office Co., Ltd. has broadened out the story that began from forest conservation issues in Japan and then spread out into global issues. The story was closed by introducing the system of More Trees, whose new products support the forest industry.

8　木は大きく2種類　針葉樹と広葉樹に分けられる

針葉樹の特徴

・生長が早い
・あまり手をかけなくてもまっすぐに伸びて育つ
・さいた部分を柱などに使いやすい
・温暖な地域の平地などに分布する

広葉樹の特徴

・生長が遅い
・枝が分かれにくく硬いものが多い
・材質が硬い
・主に家具などに使われる
・寒冷な地域や山地に分布する

11　クルミやサクラなど広葉樹の活かし方

天然林にはさまざまな広葉樹が生えています。中でも樹齢が数十年と短く、繁殖力の強いクルミは種子を多く実らせます。この種子に含まれる成分が周りの木の生長を妨げてしまうため、成熟した木の人の手で適正な時期に伐ることが求められる場合があります。

また、山間の斜面に生えてくるサクラは空に向かって上へと伸びようとするため、必然的に根元が大きく曲がってしまいます。サクラは寿命が短くして枠かれ、伐られた後、チップとして利用される木は、燃料や紙の原料になることがほとんど。実は広葉樹にも原料として利用されずにたくさんあるもったいない木がたくさんあるのです。

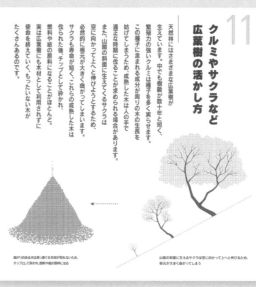

曲がりのあるまっすぐな木材が取れないため、チップとして紙の原料や燃料の原料になる

山間の斜面に生えるサクラは空に向かって上へと伸びるため、根元が大きく曲がってしまう

1　日本は国土の67%が森林である

太古から日本人は森林を大切に守り、森林とともに生きてきました。

実は、日本には手つかずの『原生林』はそれほどありません。かつて先人たちは森林から薪や木炭、食糧を採ることで、結果的に木の世代交代をうながしてきました。つまり森林の資源を人が適切に得ることで、森林のバランスは保たれてきたのです。

これが日本における典型的な「天然林」です。いま、日本は先進国の中ではフィンランドに次ぐ、世界第2位の森林保有国となっています。

74% フィンランド　67% 日本　67% スウェーデン　64% 韓国　48% ロシア

先進国の中の森林保有国 上位5ヶ国

国土面積　● 森林面積

日本全国の森林分布図。森林面積は約2500万haにおよぶ
※土地利用調整総合支援ネットワークシステム国土交通省国土・水資源局のデータを元に〔...〕再編集し作成した図を引用

2　日本の森林は40%が人工林である

天然林にはさまざまな樹種や樹齢の木々が生えています。その一方で、ひとつの樹種だけを集中的に植えて（植え替えて）人工的につくった森林を「人工林」と言います。これは木材利用を目的につくった、言わば木を生産するための畑と言えるでしょう。

日本では戦後の高度経済成長期に人工林の拡大が盛んに進められ、スギやヒノキ、カラマツなど針葉樹の単一林が森林全体の半分近くを占めるようになりました。

天然林面積 約1500万ha **60%**　　人工林面積 約1000万ha **40%**

森林面積 約2500万ha **67%**　国土面積 約3800万ha

日本の国土に対する森林面積と、天然林・人工林面積の割合。人工林面積は国土の25%を占める

16　森林が吸収したCO_2を再び放出させないために

木は太陽の光を利用して光合成を行い、CO_2（二酸化炭素）と水を吸収して炭水化物をつくり、酸素を放出しています。このような生長過程で、木が体にCO_2を取り込むことを「炭素固定」と言います。

木を伐った後に木材として利用している限りは、木の中に固定された炭素はそのまま残りますが、燃やすと再びCO_2を放出してしまいます。

森林を手入れすることで、木は盛んに光合成を行うようになるため、CO_2の吸収量が高まります。木を間伐した木を燃やしたりプロダクトとして有効利用すれば、CO_2の放出を抑えることなく有効利用することができるのです。

O_2　C 炭素　C 炭素　太陽の光　CO_2　O_2　二酸化炭素　光合成　酸素　水　水分　炭水化物

木を使った後も、木の中にある炭素は固定されたまま

木を燃やすと炭素は空気中の酸素と結びつき、二酸化炭素となって出ていく

木は葉で光合成を行い、空気中の二酸化炭素と根から吸い上げた水で、養分となる炭水化物をつくる

14　どれだけ排出しているの？　CO_2排出量を算出

私たちはどれだけのCO_2（二酸化炭素）を排出しているか知っていますか？

日本政府の発表によると、日本人1人当たり年間で約10トンのCO_2を排出しています。これは企業や工場が排出しているCO_2も含めての平均値。もう少し分かりやすく排出しているCO_2だけに絞ると、1人当たり1日約6kg。

日常生活の中で排出するCO_2は主に電気、ガス、灯油に起因します。移動のために利用する公共交通機関や自動車などからの排出量も意外に多く、全体の約4割を占めます。

例えば、ここ東京・六本木へ足を運ぶまでの交通手段を算出してみました。

電車　都営地下鉄大江戸線　乗車距離 4.8km　CO_2=0.087kg

電車　東京モノレール、都営地下鉄大江戸線　国際線→六本木　乗車距離 20.1km　CO_2=0.382kg

飛行機　高知空港→羽田空港　乗車距離 632.7km　CO_2=68.335kg

自動車　八王子市内中央自動車道→アクラスビル　乗車距離 48.8km　CO_2=7.675kg

徒歩　六本木駅→アクラスビル　乗車距離 0.8km　CO_2=0kg

新宿駅　六本木駅　羽田空港　高知空港　八王子市

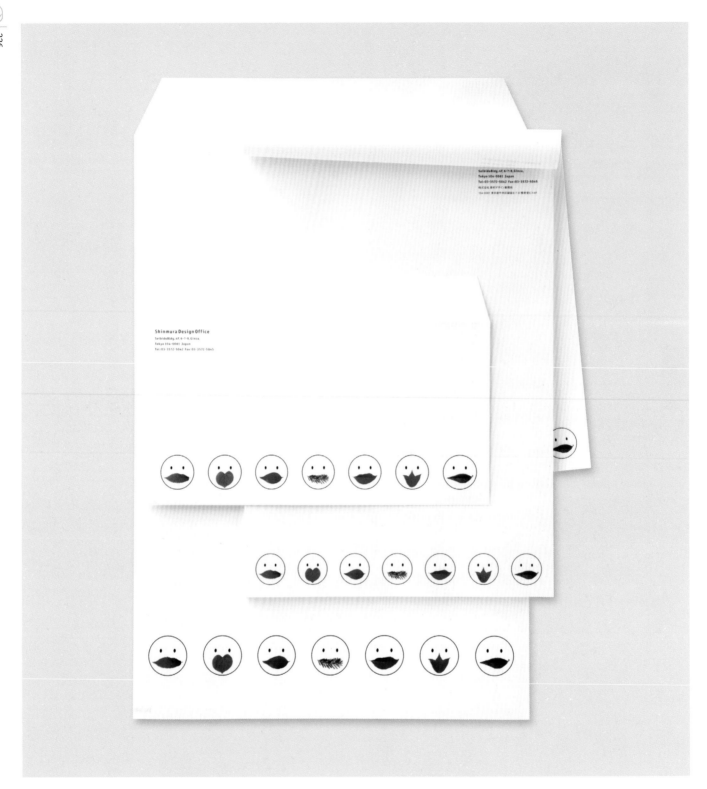

Green Smile

Design Agency Shinmura Design Office Designer Norito Shinmura Photographer Kogo Inoue

Green Smile was Norito Shinmura's back up design concept for a presentation he gave. The idea focused on giving leaves, which can't usually speak, a voice. It turned out that his plan A idea was chosen for the presentation at that time. However, the Green Smile concept could not be abandoned. Norito Shinmura became very attached to it and turned it into the identity for his design office. The image appears not only on the business cards and letterheads of Shinmura Design, but also on other things such as the face of a watch, and is gradually gaining wide use on Muji Campsite posters. At present, there are fifty-four variations of the Green Smile, each one with a unique personality based on the shape of the leaf used for the mouth.

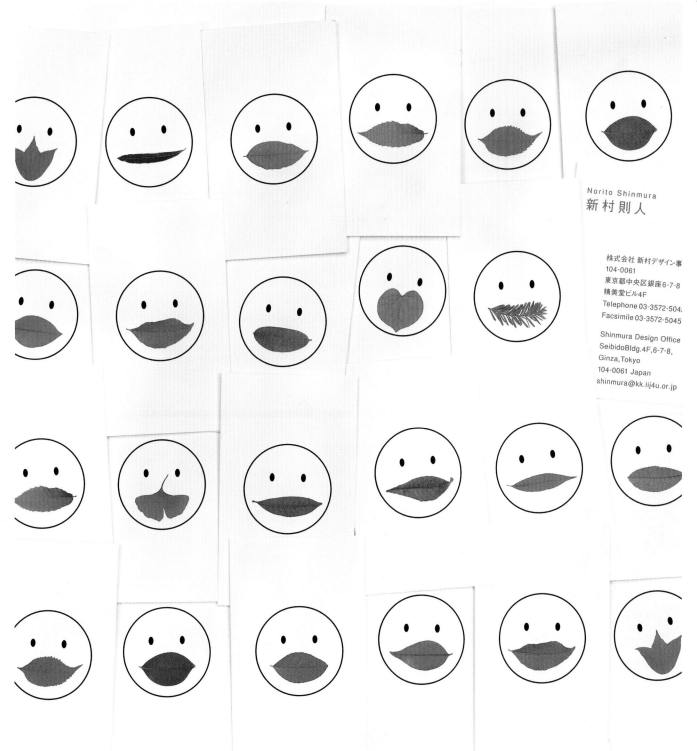

Norito Shinmura
新村則人

株式会社 新村デザイン事
104-0061
東京都中央区銀座6-7-8
精美堂ビル4F
Telephone 03-3572-504
Facsimile 03-3572-5045

Shinmura Design Office
SeibidoBldg.4F,6-7-8,
Ginza,Tokyo
104-0061 Japan
shinmura@kk.iij4u.or.jp

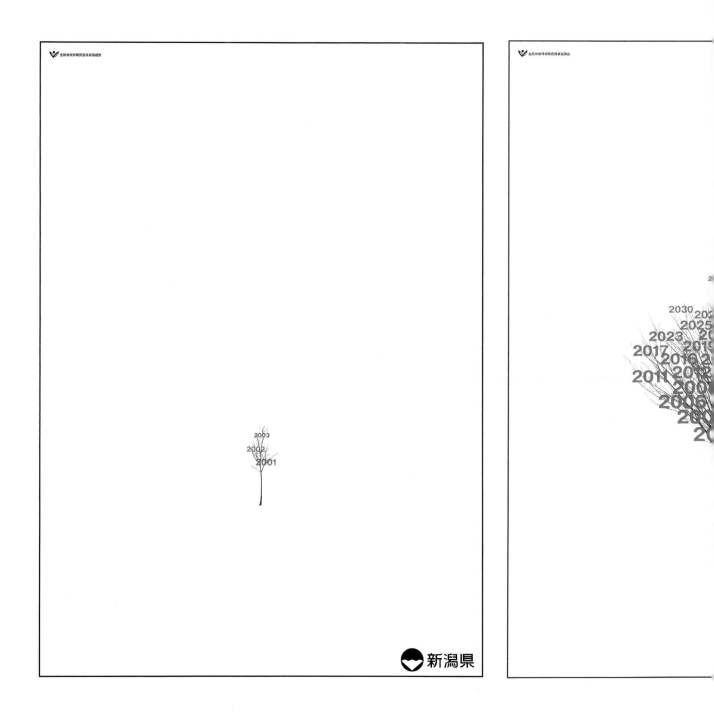

Nurturing the 21st CenTREE

Design Agency Shinmura Design Office Designer Norito Shinmura Copywriter Masakazu Nifuji Photographer Ko Hosokawa Client Niigata prefecture

The 20th century has ended and human beings have acquired many tools for easy living, but have lost many important things as well: beautiful scenery, clean air, and a generous heart. People should be more considerate of nature, which is why Shinmura Design Office started the project "100 years of greenery in Niigata prefecture". Citizens of Niigata will use the 100 years of the 21st century to plant trees and nurture them with each and every person in the community's help. This will be a wonderful legacy of greenery for children of the 22th century.

全国地域総合開発促進協議会

2100 2099
2098 2096
2098 2094 2093 2097 2091 2095
2089 2087 2088 2086 2090
2085 2084 2081 2083 2082
2074 2078 2077 2079 2080 2076
2068 2072 2070 2073 2075 2071
2060 2065 2067 2064 2069 2065 2063
2058 2059 2056 2059 2054 2057
2052 2049 2051 2048 2053 2052 2050
2045 2041 2039 2046 2047 2044 2042
2037 2038 2040 2043 2032
2030 2031 2036 2033 2035 2034 2027
2023 2022 2026 2024 2020
2017 2019 2016 2015 2014 2018
2011 2012 2010 2009 2013
2006 2004 2003 2005
2002 2001

21世木を育てます。

まもなく終わろうとしている20世紀。振り返れば、私たちは、豊かな生活を手に入れた代わりに、地球を傷つけ、多くの自然を失ってしまいました。

今、私たちは、人間の生存の基盤である自然、とりわけ清らかな空気、美しい風景など、様々な恵みをもたらしてくれる緑を取り戻すべきではないでしょうか。

そのため、新潟県民は、21世紀百年をかけて県民ひとりひとりの手で木を植え、育て、22世紀の人々に「緑の遺産」を残す

「にいがた「緑」の百年物語―木を植える県民運動」に取り組むことにしました。中国に「前人栽樹、後人涼」ということわざがあります。

百年をかけ緑を残します。22世紀のふるさと新潟の人たちのために。そして、かけがえのない地球のために。

『にいがた「緑」の百年物語―木を植える県民運動』をはじめます。

この広告に関するご意見・ご感想をお待ちしています。〒950-8570 新潟市新光町4-1 新潟県広報広聴課まで。TEL.025-280-5013 FAX.025-283-2274 http://www.pref.niigata.jp/

21世紀の木は、
22世紀の森になります。

COMES NATURALLY

COMES NATURALLY

COMES NATURALLY

COMES NATURALLY

COMES NATURALLY

COMES NATURALLY

COMES NATURALLY

COMES NATURALLY

COMES NATURALLY

Comes Naturally

Designer Junio Nguyen Gia Hai

The project was to design a set of guerrilla style advertisements for Muji Singapore. Muji is distinguished by its design minimalism, emphasis on recycling, avoidance of waste in production and packaging, and no-logo or "no-brand" policy. Muji's success is attributed to good word of mouth, a simple shopping experience, and the anti-brand movement.

Summer Sale

Design Agency Shinmura Design Office Designer Norito Shinmura Copywriter Hiroyuki Koyama Photographer Kogo Inoue Client MUJI

Memories of summer are packed into the bags framed against natural greenery.

& SMITH
www.andsmithdesign.com

Based in East London, & SMITH is a small design studio passionate about the craft and value of design. & SMITH work closely with their clients to achieve a full understanding of their business, ensuring that the work they produce engages and inspires their audience. Their work encompasses corporate identity, branding, print, web solutions, book design, signage and packaging. & SMITH believe that being small and independent gives them the opportunity to provide each of their clients with the hands-on attention to detail they deserve, and because there are no middlemen involved, their clients work directly with the designers from day one.

601bisang
www.601bisang.com

601bisang is a creative group aiming for youthful, open-minded design solutions. The designers have years of combined experience working to satisfy a truly diverse clientele range from Samsung, LG, Amorepacific, etc corporate, PyeongChang Winter Olympic 2018, and Expo 2012 Yeosu Korea, to government public relations work and design services. 601bisang's designers not only work for clients, they also realize their own design interests, create publications, and participate in exhibitions worldwide.

Amit Sakal
www.amitsakal.com

Amit Sakal is a graphic designer from Israel. He received a Bachelor's degree in design and visual communication from Shenkar College of Engineering and Design, and went on to found a small design studio in 2011. The studio specializes in identity design, logos, typography, books, catalogues, brochures, and design for the music industry.

Ampersand Creative Agency, LLC
www.ampersandca.ru

If you ask what Ampersand Creative Agency is, there is no definitive answer. The studio is composed of thinkers, doers, believers, creators, and advertisers. The designers of the studio believe in making things greater than they are; they distinguish between the good and the great, a skill evident in each project. Ampersand C. A. was founded in 2011 by graphic designer Natalia Churina and entrepreneur Milena Stoykova. Started as a small company consisting of just three people, in two years the agency successfully completed more than fifty interesting projects, built up strong relationships with partners all over the world, and met talented people with whom they continue to work as a team. Ampersand deals with brand strategy, brand development, advertising support, website creation, interactive IT projects and navigation systems.

Andrea Ataz
www.cargocollective.com/andreaataz

After studying secondary arts education, Andrea Ataz received a Graphic Design degree in Murcia, Spain. She received one of the highest marks for her final year project, La Ciudad de las Personas. She did not stop working after finishing her degree. Instead, she designed a fashion magazine, kept working as a freelance designer, and received the Leonardo da Vinci scholarship to complete a graphic design internship in Belgium. Her projects have been published in the most important annual graphic design publications in Europe.

Andrews&Co.
www.andrewsand.co

Andrews&Co. is a Geraldton based boutique design consultancy. The handpicked team of award winning design professionals from across the globe works hard to achieve creative excellence in every project they undertake. They design seamlessly across all mediums and formats, including print, screen, and environment. They are committed to craftsmanship, imagination, and goodness and create consistently beautiful and unique designs that are inspired by the regional areas in which they work.

ANONIWA
www.anoniwa.com

ANONIWA was established by the art director and designer Naoto Kitaguchi in 2009. ANONIWA focuses primarily on design for famous brands and shops, corporate identity design, visual identities, logos, branding, graphic design, book cover design, packaging design, and advertisements.

artless Inc.
www.artless.co.jp

"artless Inc." is an interdisciplinary design company that operates within a global marketplace from Tokyo, Japan. Established in 2000 by Shun Kawakami, the offices are located in Tokyo (the headquarters of the company), Kyoto, New York, London, Paris, Firenze, Helsinki and Taipei. Their activities are within the visual communication and language areas of design, which includes brand design, visual identity and corporate identity, advertising, packaging, web design, product, architecture, and sign design, etc. The designers believe in "Design as a Visual Language," and they explore within the realm "between art and design." artless manifests a diverse practice, and the many different experiences of the designers gives the agency a broader perspective on design.

asatte design office
astt.jp

asatte design office is a design office based in Japan that was founded by Satoshi Kondo. "asatte" means "the day after tomorrow" in Japanese, and the agency's graphic projects and communication champion a better future. Satoshi Kondo was born in Osaka, Japan in 1976. After graduating from Kobe University and Inter Medium Institute, he worked at Ken Miki & Associates before establishing his own office in Kobe in 2010. He has been a part time lecturer at Kobe Design University since 2011.

Atipus
www.atipus.com

Atipus is a graphic communication studio that was founded in Barcelona in 1998. The studio is made up of a team of professionals trained in various disciplines: corporate identity, art direction, packaging design, and web services. Their aim is to communicate simply through good graphic design.

BLOW
www.blow.hk

BLOW is a Hong Kong based design studio founded by Ken Lo in 2010. Specialized in branding, identity, packaging, environmental graphics, print, publications and website design, they provide clients with mind-blowing design in a simple and bold style that helps the brand to stand out in the crowd.

Bold Stockholm
www.boldstockholm.se

Bold is a strategic and multidisciplinary design agency located in Stockholm, Sweden. The agency was founded in February of 2011 by Oskar Lübeck (CD) and Carl-Fredrik af Sandeberg (CEO), together with the advertising agency Åkestam Holst. Bold's focus is building strong brands through insight driven strategy and creative design, and in its second year it was already ranked one of the top five design agencies in Sweden.

Boldincreative Pty Ltd
www.bold-inc.com

The designers of Bold-inc are passionate thinkers working within the branding and packaging industry. The studio offers down-to-earth, honest thinking that gives brands a new life and a future. They clearly understand the challenges and obstacles that brands face. Every brand and project is unique and therefore the designers don't apply a formulaic approach to their solutions. Instead they take on challenges, make bold moves, and disrupt categories (if necessary) to get the best results and deliver truly memorable designs. With a combination of creative expertise, lateral thinking, and a pinch of good old-fashioned common sense, Bold-inc prides itself on the idea: "think before we inc."

Bunch
www.bunchdesign.com

Bunch is a leading creative design studio offering a diverse range of work, including identity, literature, editorial, digital, and motion. Established in 2002 with an international reach from London to Zagreb, Bunch has an in-house team of specialists to deliver intelligent and innovative cross-platform solutions in the area of communication design. Over the years, they have been commissioned by many blue chip companies, as well as younger brands and artistic industries. They have built an impressive client base that covers many styles and disciplines, including BBC, Nike, Diesel, Sony, Sky, and Red Bull.

Caroline Morris
www.carolinemmorris.com

Caroline Morris was born and raised in Nashville, TN. She is deeply influenced by her roots in the south and finds inspiration from the culture that surrounds her. Food, vintage type, paper, music, textiles, architecture, travel, and literature all contribute to her design process. Caroline currently works for a branding agency in Birmingham, AL.

Clara Fernández
www.behance.net/cla

Clara Fernández is a young graphic designer currently studying at UBA (Buenos Aires University). She works as a freelance designer and develops personal projects. Focused on identity, editorial design, and all kinds of print design, she relishes working with illustration and typography. Clara's work is inspired by her passion for purity, simplicity and clean structured design. Fascinated with graphic design, she believes that true success depends on working with sensitivity, personality and real passion.

Commune
www.commune-inc.jp

Commune is a creative collective based in Sapporo, Japan that mainly focuses on graphic design. The theme of creation is an effort to make something better. Inspired by this will, Commune's design work may move people or make society work a little better. The Commune designers believe creating a graphic project is like giving a gift that is chosen with someone special in mind. It is a pleasure for them to be able to present something the recipient doesn't expect but truly appreciates. At times, their creations take people by surprise, awaken their emotions, or even move them to tears.

Company
www.company-london.com

Company is a design partnership in London founded in 2006 by Alex Swain and Chrysostomos Naselos. Working with a broad range of clients from individuals to institutions, they focus on visual identities, publication design, art direction, editorial and digital projects. The studio's objective is to deliver well-crafted, thoughtful, and direct design solutions. Brutal simplicity with a conceptual approach is at the heart of everything they do.

Comuniza
www.comuniza.com

Comuniza is an agency specializing in communication strategy. They believe in brand value and the power of communication. They research, analyze, consult, conceptualize, and create content oriented to the connection between brands and their communities.

Crista Conaty
www.behance.net/cpresber

Crista Conaty is a creative designer with thirteen years of experience creating digital interactive projects. She has a love of simplicity and clever design solutions.

Dalston
www.dalston.se

Dalston provides creative direction, art direction, branding and design for commercial and editorial clients within the lifestyle, fashion, retail, culture and arts worlds. Dalston wants to "challenge, simplify, and surprise." The designers of Dalston love a challenge and work with all forms of media. Among their projects are art direction for fashion, interiors, and entertainment brands and visual communication for packaging, magazines, brand identities, digital applications and exhibitions. Working with their established network of creatives, they form complete and unique workgroups to best respond to projects and client needs. This helps the agency remain flexible, and gives each and every project a unique outcome.

Dan Heron
www.danheron.co.uk

Dan Heron is a freelance graphic designer from Manchester, UK.

Daniel Berkowitz
www.danberk.prosite.com

Daniel graduated as an art director and graphic designer from the Red and Yellow school in 2001. In 2003, Dan founded SALE, the creative arm of Amperzand and Grey Cape Town that works with a variety of local and global brands. In 2007 he moved to London and spent the year freelancing at a number of agencies to fund his lust for attending a different live gig every night. Dan joined Wieden + Kennedy Delhi in 2008 as Associate Creative Director and spent three years living in the mad chaos of India and working on projects in the London and Amsterdam offices. Dan returned to Cape Town in 2012 and joined King James RSVP as Creative Director.

Danielle Shami
www.behance.net/danielleshami

Danielle Shami is a fourth year student at Shenkar Department of Visual Communication, Israel. She began her career as a photographer and participated in many competitions around the world before studying graphic design and realizing that it was her true passion. Though she specializes in motion graphics, her love of print design never dies. She applies different techniques to her projects and tries to create something new and exciting every time. Danielle loves culture, art and design and combines Decadent, Romantic and Symbolist influences within new interpretations.

David Beltran & Federica Marziale
www.behance.net/federicamarziale

David Beltran is a creative, an artist, a hippie and, most of all, a nomad. He lives in a natural and wild way; he eats flowers and falls in love with plants. Federica Marziale is a graphic designer. She walks by his side and translates ideas into something to print on paper. They have a small atelier in Milan where they spend a lot of time thinking and speaking. This is where they produce small and big ideas every day in order to make beautiful things.

Designdo Brand Design Consulting Organization
www.dd-brand.com

Designdo Brand Design Consulting Organization is a group of designers who share the same ambitions and purposes. The organization consists of partners in each brand experience. They advocate five-sense experiences as the core of a unique point of view and create brand concepts for real life design solutions. Thanks to years of in-depth brand exploration, they offer the perfect brand marketing solution for each client.

Di Suo
www.disuobookarts.com

Suo works predominantly in the medium of book arts and design, including text, images, and sometimes installations and interactive activities. Suo completed her MA with distinction at the Camberwell College of Arts in London in September of 2012. There, she discovered her strong interest in food and started to explore the potential relationship between her book projects and food-related experiences, subsequently refining her own visual and conceptual vocabulary that emerged through her focus on the points of intersection between book arts, food culture, cooking practices and reading experiences. Suo's work has been in several exhibitions in London and Kiev, as well as artists' book fairs around the UK. Her work can also be found in the Special Collections of the Chelsea College of Art and Design Library.

Diana Gibadulina.
www.behance.net/dianagibadulina

Diana Gibadulina is a Russian designer who graduated from British Higher School of Art & Design in Moscow with an emphasis on visual communication.

Dominic Rechsteiner
www.dominicrechsteiner.ch

In 2008, Dominic Rechsteiner graduated from the University of Basel with a Bachelor of Arts in visual communication.

Since then, he has worked as a freelance graphic designer. Together with friends, he founded the studio Bureau Collective in 2009. It is mainly a design studio for graphical solutions and a place where they share ideas and work on their own projects. Over the past few years he has worked with various clients, including the St. Gall Theatre, EAU-DC, and SONST.

Donna Cheng

donnacheng.co

Donna Cheng is a graphic designer and photographer originally from New York, New York, but she grew up in Connecticut. She received a Bachelor of Fine Arts in Photography from University of Connecticut and an Associates of Applied Science in Graphic Design from Parsons The New School for Design. Since graduation, she has been interning at Gabriele Wilson Design, working on book jackets and interiors. She is currently based in Jersey City, New Jersey and is enjoying her time doing what she loves as a graphic designer. Her interest lies in publication design, posters, book covers, and web design, and she constantly looks for inspiration around her. In the future, Donna hopes someday to open her own design studio in New York City.

Elixir Design Inc.

elixirdesign.com

Founded in 1992 by Jennifer Jerde, Elixir is a San Francisco-based brand identity firm specializing in holistic communication including corporate identity, marketing collateral, direct mail, packaging, and web design. The studio also helps clients with re-thinking and refining their branding and market position. This team of brand strategists, designers, writers, photographers and illustrators is culturally predisposed to create results for clients by helping them communicate honestly with their customers.

EPB - Espacio Paco Bascuñán

www.espaciopacobascunan.com

EPB is a small graphic design studio in Valencia, Spain that is focused on identity, brand, and website design. EPB makes books, curates exhibitions, and has a beautiful garden. The studio has offices in both Valencia and Barcelona and the people in charge of it are Lupe Martínez, Bea Bascuñán and Albert Jornet. They consider design a way of life and thinking and try to express that in every project.

Erika Ko

www.kimchee.uk.com

Erika Ko is a branding specialist and graphic designer, originally from Korea and now based in London. After graduating from Kingston University with an MA in Communication Design and the Creative Economy, she became involved in a number of retail graphic design and commercial branding projects. A keen foodie, she has shown talent in creative design within the hospitality sector and currently works as the in-house designer at Wasabi Co. Ltd, where the Director, Mr. Dong Hyun Kim, has a keen eye for design and changing trends in the food industry. Wasabi currently has 31 branches throughout London and New York. Erika Ko was instrumental in the creation of the branding.

Esther Rieser

estherrieser.ch

Esther Rieser is a Swiss graphic designer based in Zurich, who works with a range of clients from individuals to institutions. Her focus is on printed matter, including editorial design, publication design, exhibition title design, and visual identity. The studio's approach focuses on research and conceptual thinking.

Estudi Conrad Torras

www.conradtorras.com

Estudi Conrad Torras specializes in graphic design and communication, with extensive experience in corporate identity, packaging, signage, publishing, photography, and web design. The studio is very involved in each project in order to achieve the best results; their designs work and are adaptable to each client's needs and resources. The studio's projects are the result of a rational and creative effort that places special importance on functionality in order to offer a good final product. A differentiating touch is applied to all projects to achieve superior results. Estudi Conrad Torras emphasizes maintaining good communication with clients in order to offer a first rate final project. Estudi Conrad Torras is open to new challenges, implementing research and hard work to achieve optimal results.

Estúdio Alice

estudioalice.com.br

Alice is a hybrid of good plus evil, right and wrong, Coke and Menthos, yin and yang, Monty Python and *The Godfather*. Alice is pragmatic sum, but creative resolution. It's a studio of six people. United by their affinities, the designers strive to create through differences. Every day is more than simply working or being a professional whatever. Each activity is shared to exercise the idea of a true studio. Is it work!? Yes, but it's gotta be fun. It ain't worth it if it ain't fun. It's part of our instruction manual. Alice wants inspiration. Alice works conceptually. Alice makes it real by being fun. Alice likes to discuss possibilities and strategies. Alice likes buzz words. Alice likes colorful drawings. Alice wants life to have more in it.

Frost Design

frostdesign.com.au

Frost lives and breathes design, working across all touch points to deliver the audience your brand deserves. They help companies like yours hone a message that cuts through with clarity to deliver a competitive edge. From commerce to charity, education to leisure, they are inspiring ideas to life through simple, simply brilliant design.

Grid

www.gridworldwide.com

Grid is a design and branding company that approaches the design process with good strategic thinking. Their core team is chosen for their creativity, commitment, and approach to solving complicated problems. Good design is not about capturing a fad or trend; it's about timelessness, creating a product that's as current in 100 years as it is today. Good design doesn't stand up, wave its arms and scream "look at me" — it blends naturally into your world, not interrupting but enriching it.

Hardhat Design

www.hardhatdesign.co.uk

Hardhat is a friendly creative studio founded in 2000 by Nickolus Clifford and Jenny Miles, who have been working together in various forms for 13 years. They produce the vast majority of the studio's work themselves but call on a wide network of other creative minds when a job requires it. With bases in London, UK, and Auckland, NZ, Hardhat continues to nurture their growing list of clients from home and as far and wide as New York, Paris, Melbourne, Delhi & Accra. Along with their wide ranging skills across many different mediums, Hardhat always strives to gain a genuine understanding of their clients. The studio has an ongoing aim for excellence in all it does, whether branding, print, web, or email marketing. The Hardhat designers also pride themselves on being able to be well and truly hands-on right from the very first idea through to final delivery.

Inbal Lapidot

www.cargocollective.com/inbaloza

Inbal Lapidot is a fourth year visual communication student at Holon Institute of Technology, Israel. As long as she can remember, she has had an interest, vivid curiosity, and passion for design and art. Inbal seeks inspiration in everything around her, from fashion and textiles to photography, illustration, magazines and books. Her view is that our ability to reach out and communicate with anyone is important, and her favorite niche of communication is the visual one: the ability to enhance a verbal message through visual means. With every passing day, design is becoming an ever more integral part of Inbal's life.

Interabang

www.interabang.uk.com

Interabang is a London design agency that was founded by Adam Giles and Ian McLean.

Intraligi

www.intraligi.com

Studio Intraligi was founded ten years ago by Philippe Intraligi and is based on the principle of following one's dreams. In the time since Philippe founded the studio, he has traveled across the globe to learn from and collaborate with some of the most creative people in the fields of advertising, corporate design and fashion. He worked at MetalDesign and adidas originals in Germany, Leagas Delaney in Italy, and Li-Ning in China. Now based in New York, Philippe has proven himself to be ready for any challenge; he continually creates outstanding design solutions for clients including IBM, Citiband, Uniqlo, and Rocawear.

Jessica Comingore

jessicacomingore.com

Jessica Comingore is a designer and photographer living and working in Los Angeles, California. A graduate of The Fashion Institute of Design & Merchandising, Jessica began her career working for established interior design firms throughout Los Angeles, managing residential and commercial projects, overseeing marketing, and contributing to the design and development of a line of textiles. Through her extensive exposure to high-end design and architecture, coupled with a keen eye for detail, Jessica discovered her passion for photography and began shooting interiors for reputable designers throughout Southern California. In 2011, Jessica Comingore Studio was born, combining her design experience with her love for photo taking, allowing her to work with a range of creative clients, from local entrepreneurs to international publications. Jessica brings a refined sensibility to projects for clients in areas of branding, packaging, print, and web, along with interior photography and art direction. Aside from running her design studio, Jessica also pens her own lifestyle blog, founded in 2007.

Jessica Pitcher

www.jessicapitcher.com

Jessica Pitcher is a recent Visual Communication Honours graduate living and working in Melbourne.

Juliette Cezzar

juliettecezzar.com

Juliette Cezzar is a designer, educator, and author based in New York City. She is currently the Director of the BFA Communication Design and BFA Design & Technology programs at Parsons / The New School. She holds an MFA in Graphic Design from Yale University and a professional degree in Architecture from Virginia Tech. She established her small studio, e.a.d., in 2005, after her second year-long stint as a freelance designer at the Museum of Modern Art.

Junio Nguyen Gia Hai

www.j-junio.com

Junio Nguyen Gia Hai was born in Saigon, Vietnam and now lives in Singapore to focus on his career. He just finished his BA in Design Communication with a major in Advertising and Graphic at LASALLE, College of the Arts (Honors), Second Upper Class. Junio loves advertising and design because of the mixture of ideas that can work in a practical context. He is a thinker who visualizes all his ideas. As a designer, environment plays an important part in his world of inspirations. He picks up ideas from every single aspect of everyday life.

K & K Designbuero

www.kuk-designbuero.de

K & K is a small design studio in the heart of Munich, Germany. Manuela Weiss and Nadine Wittmann stand for comprehensive and consistent solutions concerning brand concepts and communication materials (both print and online). The basis of their creative mode of operation is passion and enthusiasm. The name "KLECKERN & KLOTZEN" originates from a German saying. Figuratively it means that K&K is always interested in new challenges, big and small.

Kenichi Matsumoto

e-ltd.co.jp

Kenichi Matsumoto was born in 1980 in Tokyo. He graduated from the Department of Graphic Design at Tama Art University and joined E. Co., Ltd. in 2004. Kenichi received many awards, including Best Work

Bronze in Graphics from the Japan Typography Association Awards (2011), One Show Design (2009), One Show Design Merit (2010, 2011, and 2012), NY ADC Young Gun 8 (2010). His work has also won awards in JAGDA, TDC, and ADC and the Japan Package Design Award.

KentLyons

www.kentlyons.com

Formed in 2003, KentLyons is a team of designers and developers based in London. They focus on creating communications that are simultaneously beautiful and useful. Their work wins many awards and is highly effective and moving. The team is made up of Design, Visual Communications, Arts and Computer Science experts. They produce effortlessly elegant books or intuitive iPad reading experiences with the same ease. They create clear, compelling ideas, and communicate them with style, simplicity and passion.

Kipo Design Group

www.kipo.name

Kipo Design Group consists of Kirill Belyaev and Polina Oshurkova, designers from Saint Petersburg, Russia. They are impressed and inspired by minimalist, inexpensive decisions that are at the same time intellectual and, more importantly, functional. They are active in different fields of design and admire Scandinavian and Japanese industrial design and architecture. The designers in the group create names and concepts, website designs, corporate identities, illustrations, print materials, and photographs.

Kota Kobayashi

kotakobayashi.com

Kota is a multi-disciplinary designer based in New York. He utilizes the marketing skills that he gained in the United States and the delicate sensibility of Japanese culture in his design. His work has been recognized by multiple international design awards. He is now with Huge in Brooklyn.

Laura J. Merriman

behance.net/lauramerriman

Laura J. Merriman grew up with a rowdy family of six in the small town of Wabash, IN. She

currently is a senior graphic design student from Ball State University with a BFA in Visual Communication and a minor in Landscape Architecture. Her favorite pastimes are traveling, reading, and eating. She is working toward a life in the design field that suits both her graphic and architecture backgrounds.

Lisa Hedge

www.lisahedge.com

Lisa Hedge is a graphic designer, illustrator, and art director originally from New Zealand and currently based in New York. She encountered graphic design while studying arts at the University of Southern California and has pursued a number of professional experiences in both fields since. Various highlights include an internship as a painting assistant at Takashi Murakami's New York studio, Kaikai Kiki, working as gallery assistant to the curator and art dealer Lynn del Sol at CTS Creative rift shop, and as a designer for an array of brands at design studios and creative agencies such as Khiel's, Tender Creative and Partners & Spade.

Lo Siento

www.losiento.net

Lo Siento is a small studio that creates entire concepts for identity projects. The main feature of their process is an organic and physical approach to solutions, resulting in a field where graphic and industrial design have dialogue within the search for an alliance with artisan processes.

Longton

longtondesign.com

Longton is a design studio based in Melbourne, Australia. They provide clients around the world with design and art direction services that garner attention and show purpose.

Lucas Rampazzo

lucasrampazzo.com

Lucas Rampazzo is a graphic designer, visual artist, and musician from Brazil, São Paulo. In 2011, he completed an artist residency in Rotterdam/ NL at Hommes Gallery with a wallpaper project and a music piece. As a graphic designer, Lucas develops work in various segments such as editorial, fashion, video, music, package, visual identity, and print design, among others. As an introspective observer, he tries to take in music, purity, beauty and simplicity as design inspiration.

Maite Elias Uria
www.maidesign.es

Maite studied Advertising and Communication at the University of the Basque Country (Bilbao). Graphic design became her main interest after she started at the University and tried out different courses. After graduating, Maite had an internship at an Advertising Agency for two months and ended up working there for two more years. For that job, she managed and worked on the biggest campaigns, including all types of graphic design projects. She subsequently switched to a more professional design studio, working in branding for different companies, with closer contact with customers. Finally, she decided to develop a new business of her own, and Mai Design was created! The fresh new studio creates advertisements and branding for all kind of companies like Lonjan, a well-known surfboard & clothing company.

Malin Holmstrom
www.malinholmstrom.com

Malin Holmstrom is a Swedish graphic designer based in Stockholm. Her career started in Stockholm, where she went to the renowned Berghs School of Communications and was granted the opportunity to finish her studies in Sydney, Australia. In Sydney, she received her bachelor degree, was Graduate of the Year runner-up, and received the Shine Award. Since graduating, she has worked for Landor Sydney, Interbrand Sydney, and Landor Paris, with clients such as AGDA, the City of Melbourne, Diageo, GWF, Orange, P&G, and Telstra. Malin's work has received numerous awards and has been recognized by several books and blogs.

MARC&ANNA
www.marcandanna.co.uk

MARC&ANNA was set up in 2005 by Marc Atkinson and Anna Ekelund. The directors both graduated from Central Saint Martins College of Art & Design in 2001 and went on to work for high-profile design agencies before setting up MARC&ANNA. They have a strong belief in what they do. The designers help clients communicate their message clearly and intelligently, create beautiful work with strong ideas, and deliver end results beyond expectation on all projects and with all budgets.

Marina Company
www.mirindacompany.com

Marina is the winner of over 40 national and international awards, including four prizes at the international graphic design red dot awards in Essen, a Fab award in London, four best pack awards in Spain, ten bronze Laus, seven silver trophy Laus, and three gold trophy Laus. Marina founded Mirinda Company in 2005, where she works as an art director and graphic designer. She designs projects where creativity is a priority applied to any medium: advertising, packaging, graphic design, and so on. An atmosphere of communication with the client throughout the process is an important element of each design. Every strategy is a creative process. It must open new paths instead of closing doors. It is crucial that designers and clients all work together toward the same goal, within an atmosphere of confidence and collaboration.

Marta Afonso
www.behance.net/martaafonso

Marta Afonso is a multidisciplinary designer and illustrator. Her academic career began with a Degree in Design from the University of Aveiro (Portugal). She then attended the University of Fine Arts in Barcelona (Spain) and is now finishing her Masters Degree in Communication Design at the School of Arts and Design in Porto. Marta develops her own projects and works as a freelancer. She enjoys getting involved in projects of social awareness in order to call into question stereotypes and visual conventions of representation.

Matt Willey
www.mattwilley.co.uk

Matt graduated from Central St. Martins in 1997. After gaining valuable experience at a handful of small design companies, he joined the internationally acclaimed studio Frost Design, later becoming Creative Director. In 2005, he co-founded Studio8 Design with Zoë Bather. Matt is a co-founder and co-creative director of Port Magazine, which launched in February of 2011. Matt is on the board of the Editorial Design Organization and is the Vice Chairman of The Typographic Circle. He is an external examiner for The University of Lincoln design course and is a visiting lecturer at Skolen for Visuel Kommunikation in Denmark. Matt has won various honors for his work, including two Premier Awards from the International Society of Typographic Designers, Silver Awards from the Society of Publications Designers and The Art Directors Club, and a Platinum Award from Graphis, as well as recognition from D&AD, The Design Week Awards, The Type Directors Club, and AIGA.

Maykol Medina
www.maikoru.com

Growing up in Charallave & Caracas, Venezuela, Maykol was always interested in other cultures and in Chinese, Arabic, and Nepalese characters, but it wasn't until he moved to Kyoto that his knowledge of Chinese characters became so strong that he started to experiment with them in a more conceptual and artistic way. Maykol Medina calls himself a graphic expressionist, because he thinks he is not completely a graphic designer or completely an artist, but instead functions somewhere between these two titles.

Mot
www.motstudio.com

Mot, a multi-disciplinary design studio based in Barcelona, was founded by Laia Clos in 2006. Working with a variety of clients, Mot's work ranges from small private commissions to public corporate identities and large publications. The studio's mission is to treat each project with the same care and attentiveness in order to produce sensitive, functional design while working in close collaboration with clients. The studio's designers take pleasure in developing concept driven work and pay great attention to detail and craft.

Nae-Design
www.nae-design.com

Nae-Design is an award-winning Sydney studio providing brand identity and digital design solutions. "Nae" means "young plants" in Japanese and creative director and former stem-cell neuroscientist Dr. Nae West is especially fond of plants.

Nakano Design Office Co., Ltd.
nakano-design.com

Takeo Nakano graduated from Musashino Art University Department of Visual Communication Design in 2001. He started his career at Katsui Design Office and in 2011 established Nakano Design Office Co.,Ltd. Takeo has won prizes like "Applied Typography" Grand Prix and "Best Work" and the "CS Design Award" Merit Award. He is also a lecturer at Musashino Art University, Tama Art University, and MeMe Design School.

Nicholas Jeeves
www.nicholasjeeves.com

Nicholas Jeeves was born in 1972 and educated at Kingshott School and Hitchin Boys' School. He graduated from Cambridge School of Art in 1994 with a degree in Graphic Arts and Illustration and spent the early part of his career designing some of the UK's earliest commercial websites, as well as print projects for clients including The Royal Albert Hall and Virgin Publishing. After five years developing his career as an independent designer, in 2000 Nicholas was invited back to Cambridge to teach as a visiting lecturer and has continued there ever since. He has tutored young designers at the University of Bedfordshire, Milan's Accademia di Comunicazione, and Ankara's Baskent University, as well as helping to develop D&AD's Student Awards brief and serving on its jury. In January of 2012, Nicholas enrolled in the Applied Imagination masters degree at Central St. Martins, London, with a goal of using text and image as a way of investigating more complex ideas of storytelling, mythology, and religion under the name Nicholas of Hitchin.

Norito Shinmura

www.shinmura-d.co.jp

Norito Shinmura was born in Japan in 1960, the youngest of eight siblings in a fisherman's family. After stints at Shin Matsunaga Design and I&S/BBDO, Norito established Shinmura Design Inc. His major clients include Shiseido, Ryohin Keikaku (MUJI Campground, BGM), Tokyo Olympics Candidature File, and Sapporo Breweries. Numerous awards demonstrate his career success, like the Mainichi Advertising Design Award (Grand Prix), Grand Prize in the Environmental Advertising Contest Award, Bronze Prize from the Tokyo Type Directors, a Good Design Award, and Silver and Bronze prizes from the New York Art Directors Club Awards.

Nuri Cha

www.nuricha.com

Nuri Cha is a graphic designer based in New York City who loves the colors and patterns of nature, Central Park, and anything typographic. She also loves to paint and work on printed matter, identity designs, and environmental graphics.

Olssøn Barbieri

www.olssonbarbieri.com

Olssøn Barbieri, formerly known as DesignersJourney, is a multi-disciplinary design agency specializing in brand identity and packaging design, with particular focus on wine/ spirits, luxury items, fashion, culture, and arts industries. Founded with the intention of working independently and without compromise in regard to conceptual development and the quality of execution, the company evolves by pursuing new standards of design through research and experimentation. The company's projects range from brand creation, visual identity, illustration, and packaging design to brand design strategy and creative direction. Olssøn Barbieri was founded in 2005 by Henrik Olssøn and Erika Barbieri, whose works have been published and awarded by national and international juries.

Oriol Gil

www.behance.net/oriolgil

Oriol Gil was born in 1976 in Barcelona, Spain. He studied Graphic Design in the Escola Massana of arts and crafts, where he was in contact with other art disciplines like photography, sculpture, and painting. After graduation, he worked for a year with an independent photographer and learned about photography techniques. In 1998, he started work at El Sindicato, a small creative advertising agency with clients including Audi and Bombay Gin. After four years at El Sindicato, he worked for two years at Arnold Spain doing art direction for Panasonic and Bwin. In 2007, he founded a studio called The Öwn with Nacho Ginestra. Over three years, they completed work for clients like Volkswagen, Camper, MACBA, ARO, and took on other creative projects in Barcelona. In 2010, he started a new project inside Villar-Rosás called La Forma, working for Nike, Honda, Damm Beer and many others. Since 2012, he's worked on freelance projects in the areas of graphic design, motion graphics and art direction.

P.NITTA Nutsatit

www.behance.net/pnitta

P.NITTA Nutsatit is a Bangkok-based designer focusing on brand identity, graphic and packaging. She is now a brand identity designer at Contour, Co., Ltd, a creative network that is especially concerned with brand strategy. Her role is to build up new brand visual identities in order to accomplish brand goals. In her free time, she loves doing crafts and illustration and reading books. She likes to listen to loud music while she walks. Her passion is traveling, which is a series of small adventures.

Paperview Design

www.paperviewdesign.com

PAPERVIEW is a design studio and concept lab specializing in print media. From offices in Beirut, they have collaborated with a roster of international and regional clients. The studio's services include corporate branding, identity creation and development, and multimedia design. PAPERVIEW also has a highly successful track record in the restaurant sector, with work completed for some of the most well known restaurants, lounges and clubs in the region's nightlife scene.

PAPERVIEW's clients are a broad spectrum of architects, interior designers, jewelry designers, restaurants, bars, nightclubs, hotels, universities, and beauty lounges to IT companies, NGOs, and pharmaceuticals.

Paperwhite

www.paperwhite-studio.com

Paperwhite is a multidisciplinary design studio based in New York City focusing on identity, branding, print, and interactive work. Their principals work closely with clients to make work that is smart, visually engaging and accessible to diverse audiences.

Principle Design

www.principledesign.com.au

Principle Design is a studio with a conscience. Experienced and energetic, with a collective passion for innovative communication and a practical and progressive ideology based on green design fundamentals and ethical practice. Their in-house resources are plentiful and diverse. With designers, illustrators, and photographers under one roof, the studio delivers integrated communication solutions across the full spectrum of traditional and new media applications, including identity programs, brochures, signage, annual reports and websites.

RODRIGO AGUADÉ & MANUEL ASTORGA

www.wearemast.com

Rodrigo Aguadé Studio is a boutique design agency that was founded in Paris in 2004 by Creative Director Rodrigo Aguadé. In the first few years, Rodrigo worked closely with international artists helping to develop art installations in museums such as the Centre Pompidou and the Fondation Cartier, and then later moving into the fashion field when he became art director of Soon Magazine. Since early 2011, Manuel Astorga has played a key role in the team. His experience in the advertising field and strong graphic signature combine perfectly to enhance the scope and quality of the studio's international projects.

RONCHAM DESIGN OFFICE

www.roncham.com

Roncham is brand design consultancy based in Pairs, Shanghai and Changzhou. Their services include brand strategy, corporate identity, brand identity, packaging, retail & environmental, etc. They create consumer experiences and help to improve the brand value of clients to move their businesses forward.

Rosa de Jong

www.byrosa.nl

Rosa de Jong is a freelance designer, art director, and animator based in Amsterdam. After studying commercial art direction and working for one or two agencies, she started working for her own clients. All projects made by Rosa are made to fit the client as best as possible. Since people are naturally drawn to stories that are different, the goal is to tell the real story of the brand and set it apart from the crowd, making every piece of communication authentic and personal. With uniqueness the goal, the work often is handmade or accompanied by illustrations.

Ruiyi Design Office

www.ruiyids.com

Ruiyi Design Office is an advertising and design studio in Changsha, Hunan Province, China.

Saga Mariah Design

www.sagamariahdesign.se

Saga Mariah Sandberg is a Stockholm based designer working with art direction, design, and illustration. Her work mainly includes packaging design and identities such as logotype designs, company profiles and product identities, as well as booklet design and concepts. Clients include big and small Swedish corporations such as Björn Axén, IKEA, North Kingdom, ICA, Björn Borg and Naturligtvis.

Sasha Prood

www.sashaprood.com

Sasha Prood is a designer, illustrator, and devotee of all things paper. She specializes in typography, illustration, and pattern design in the mediums of pencil, pen, and watercolor. She pursues a balance between art and design, blending work done by hand and on a computer. Sasha always has a sketchbook with her to jot down new ideas and inspiration. These days, much of her inspiration comes from science, nature, traditional cultural practices and vintage, utilitarian and childhood items. It is wonderful to be able to pursue her work based directly on what inspires her in daily life.

SeventhDesign™

www.seventhdesign.com.ar

SeventhDesign™ is a branding studio based in Buenos Aires, Argentina, creating customized and ambitious solutions for national and international clients for almost 8 years. With expertise in identity, print, packaging, interactivity, and environments, the SeventhDesign™ studio crafts initiatives that integrate multiple disciplines. Through wide-ranging capabilities and extensive reach, they coordinate programs that address the spectrum of a client's needs from a unified perspective. This work helps facilitate communication between client stakeholders, resulting in adaptable systems that define visual communication across an organization.

Shegeek Design / Seed

www.shegeekdesign.com
www.seedsf.com

Shegeek Design, based in San Francisco, California, is an award-winning graphic design and strategic branding agency. For 20 years, Shegeek has worked with corporate and lifestyle clients to extend brands across all touch points. In 2011, Shegeek Design opened Seed as an offshoot agency to focus on providing design and branding expertise to clients who create honest, artisanal pure food and honor the burgeoning social and environmental shifts taking place.

STUDIO PATTEN

studiopatten.com

Trusting in design as a starting point, Studio Patten develops and expands creative content for an aesthetic connection. Studio Patten believes in a different and connected way of working. It doesn't matter the

motive or the medium; what is important is the language of the content.

T-Square Design Associates

www.t2designassociates.jp

T-Square Design Associates is located in Tokyo and Osaka. The studio specializes in brand development and architecture. Creative director Eiji Tsuda has over 10 years of experience in design and communication. His expertise in branding and visual communication comes from two centers of cultures, New York and Tokyo. Prior to forming T-Square Design Associates, he worked as a senior designer at VSA Partners and Wolff Olins in New York, and most recently as a design director at the The Brand Union in Tokyo. He has a broad understanding of branding in both business interactions and to create end-user value. He has worked with a diverse selection of clients globally, from finance organizations, pharmaceutical companies, electronics businesses, cosmetics companies, media organizations, and major publications to non-profit organizations. His work has been featured in both national and international publications including Graphis Annuals, Black Book AR100, Communication Arts, HOW and Print magazines. He holds a B.F.A from Maryland Institute College of Art.

The Chase

thechase.co.uk

The Chase describes themselves as creative consultants. Not designers, writers, advertisers, or brand strategists but all of these and more. The Chase uses an elephant story to explain their philosophy. Once, there was an old Indian craftsman who carved the most beautiful elephants from unpromising blocks of timber. Asked how he did it, he simply replied: "I just cut away the wood that doesn't look like an elephant." In their words it means: The Chase look hard to discover what it is you want to say, focus on a core message, and then use creativity to ensure that the results are noticed.

Tomato Košir

www.behance.net/tomato

Tomato is a graphic designer,

typographer, photographer, and amateur pole bean cultivator. As a two and a half year old boy he was more interested in newspaper headlines and signs in hospital waiting rooms than walking and picking his nose, activities that his family thought were much more suitable for a boy of his age. It was around that time that his first typeface with 25 characters was created. It was drawn in the air with his fingers and was gone in an instant. Two months later, his second typeface made of crayons remained on the table until lunchtime. With his third typeface, made of potato dumplings, he poisoned himself in kindergarten at the age of three. From that time on, he was taken care of by his grandmother, uncle, German shepherd Rina, and a flock of white hens. When he was four he used one of the hens as a house pony and broke its wing. He never forgot that chicken stew. He is now a vegetarian and his work is often reminiscent of those white hens.

Turnstyle

www.turnstylestudio.com

Turnstyle is a graphic design and branding firm founded on the belief that in a crowded marketplace, people gravitate emotionally toward companies and products that project a distinctive style. In the words of French poet Jean Cocteau, "Style is a simple way of saying complex things." Design's power is in its ability to craft that stylistic distinction and to communicate on an emotional, visceral level. The firm emphasizes design execution because that's where the analytical rubber meets the emotional road. In a nutshell, they breathe life into products and businesses by infusing clever design thinking into impeccably executed materials and experiences.

Ultra:studio

www.ultrastudio.ch

Created in 2004 by Ludovic Gerber, Ultra:studio is a graphic design studio based in Vevey, Switzerland. Ultra:studio is characterized by simple and clever concepts realized through typographic design and bold colors.

Vanessa Pepin

www.behance.net/vanessapepin

Vanessa Pepin is a graphic designer from Montreal, Canada. Her design fields covers branding, typograpy, print design, web design and etc. Currently she is available for freelance jobs.

Wang Hua

www.thehuadesign.com

Wang Hua is a graphic designer, currently doing her master course at London College of Communication (UAL) in the UK. She is fond of design and likes discovering the beauty of subtle things in life. In her opinion, Chinese designers of the new generation should dedicate themselves to developing their work as truly modern and stop using old cultural elements and symbols again and again. Chinese designers should make modern design with regional character through a Chinese manner of expression.

Wang Wen

www.behance.net/abulala

Wang Wen graduated from Luxun Academy of Fine Arts and is about to go abroad to finish MFA courses in the U.S. Nature and culture are two things that she is very interested in; one is made by God and the other is made by people. She chooses her projects to show great respect for both.

Zaijia Huang

www.zaijiadesign.com

Zaijia Huang is a graphic designer originally from China but now residing in Paris, France.

Zdunkiewicz Studio

www.zdunkiewicz.pl

Zdunkiewicz Studio is one-man studio based in Warsaw, Poland, founded by graphic designer Krzysztof Zdunkiewicz. Focused on branding and print projects, Krzysztof Zdunkiewicz is an art director with seven years of experience in advertising, branding, and making projects in his own small studio in Eastern Europe. He has a great love of simplicity, clean ideas, typography, vintage elements, and black and white projects.

ACKNOWLEDGEMENTS

We would like to acknowledge our gratitude to the artists and designers for their generous contributions of images, ideas and concepts. We are very grateful to many other people whose names do not appear on the credits but who provided assistance and support. Thanks also go to people who have worked hard on the book and put ungrudging efforts into it. Without you all, the creation and ongoing development of this book would not have been possible. Thank you for sharing your innovation and creativity with all our readers.